THE WAY

WORSHIPER

Discover the

Secret to Friendship

with God

The Way of a Worshiper

Published by Maranatha!
A division of The Corinthian Group, Inc
205 Avenida Fabricante, San Clemente, CA 92672
www.maranathamusic.com

Cover design by Bradley Grose.
Interior design by Bradley Grose and Terry DeGraff

Printed in the United States of America

ISBN 0-9724274-0-6

THE FRAMEWORK

Therefore,
I urge you, brothers,
in view of God's mercy,
to offer your bodies
as living sacrifices,
holy and pleasing to God
—this is your spiritual
act of worship.
Do not conform any longer
to the pattern of this world,
but be transformed by the
renewing of your mind.
Then you will be able to test
and approve what God's will is
—his good, pleasing and
perfect will.

(Romans 12:1-2)

ONE

ARE YOU LOOKING FOR GOD?

The friendship of God is with those who fear him;
he makes known to them the secrets of his covenant.
(Psalm 25:14)[1]

Are you looking for God? Is he only rumored to exist in your world? Is it possible to really know him? If he spoke to you would you recognize his voice? Would he recognize yours?

The pursuit of God is the chase of a lifetime—in fact it's been going on since the day you were born.

The question is, have you been the hunter or the prey?

◆

I'm not an extraordinary person.

Unusual, maybe, but unusual in a very ordinary way. I don't have any horrid tales of a sordid past languishing in sin and degradation. (Although I did chase Clifford Booten down the block with a kitchen knife in my hand when I was six years old because he was flirting with a girl I liked. But other than that, there's not much worthy of the tabloids.)

I'm a middle-aged American male, married (very happily) to a woman who is much more extraordinary than I am. I have four loony kids who bring me great joy. I've lost most of my hair. I'm now growing out instead of up. I'm not wealthy. I'm not famous. I'm just an average person—probably like your next-door neighbor.

But I am a worshiper.

And I have a message for you—a message that, as Jeremiah said, "is in my heart like a fire, a fire shut up in my bones. I am weary of holding it in; indeed, I cannot" (Jer 20:9). This message comes from my own longing to know God. To know that he is really there—or really here, I should say—not just in theory, not just in feelings, either; but rather in day to day, moment by moment, living, breathing, present, absolute certainty—a certainty that is higher than intellect and deeper than emotions. I long to know him as my God. To know him as my Father. To know him as my Friend.

I've had this longing since I was a young boy. My mother still laughs about the times she found me, long after bedtime, with my head under the covers reading my Bible with a flashlight. Sometimes I think God laughs about it too.

There is a risk in saying what I am about to say. The risk is that I might sound condescending—that I will appear to have "arrived" at some deep or exalted level of spirituality that is unattainable for others; or worse yet, that I will appear to *believe* that I have arrived. But it's a risk I am willing to take. I know that neither is true. I haven't "arrived" anywhere. We are all on a journey. I'm just a friend telling a friend what I am learning along the way.

But I can honestly say today that I am continually aware of God's presence. And I am also aware of my growing hunger for more of him. I live in the paradox of having found God, or rather, of having been found by him, and yet having to always search for him. Jesus tells us that he is the Good Shepherd in search of lost sheep. But sheep, once found, spend the rest of their lives in pursuit of their shepherd, following his lead, listening for his voice.

I sense God's presence not because he decided to "show up," but because I decided to show up. I have made myself available to him by becoming a worshiper; and in so doing, I have availed myself of his open invitation to friendship.

There is something else that I am keenly aware of: I am aware of the pleasure God finds in my being present with him. It's the kind of pleasure a child senses from her father when he tells her how happy he is to see her at the end of the day. It's the kind of pleasure you sense when a friend of yours tells you how much he enjoys spending time with you. It's the pleasure you sense when you know that you are in the presence of someone who is delighted to see you.

> **The Lord delights in those who fear him,**
> **who put their hope in his unfailing love. (Psalm 147:11)**

To sense God's pleasure is a humbling, reassuring, and yet baffling experience. I know me. Why God would take pleasure in me is beyond my comprehension. But he does. In spite of my faults. In spite of my failures. In spite of my inconsistencies and insecurities. Jesus is truly the Friend of sinners (Mt 11:19). I know it just as surely as I know that I am saved.

You can live in God's pleasure too. You can know his continual presence. God has no favorite children. There are no specially privileged citizens in the kingdom. We all have equal access to the lap of the Father and to the throne of the King.

The way of a worshiper is never traveled alone, because a worshiper is God's constant companion. Psalm 25:14 says, "The friendship of God is with those who fear him." What does it mean to fear the Lord? Matthew Henry, the great 17th century theologian, wrote that to fear the Lord is to "stand in awe of his majesty and worship him with reverence, submit to his authority and obey him with cheerfulness, dread his wrath and [be] afraid of offending him."[2]

What I have to share with you in these pages is what I am learning about being a worshiper. This little book is built on the framework of Romans 12:1-2. The chapters are divided into three sections. In the first section, we will examine God's mercy and what it means to be holy and acceptable to God. In the second section, we will consider the difference between conforming and being transformed, why God wants our bodies, and what it means to live as a sacrifice. In the third section, we will discover what it means to have a renewed mind, and how to enjoy deep friendship with God by "reading his mind and praying his thoughts."

I've used a lot of scripture in this book. I find that every time I speak on these topics, I am asked for a list of my Scripture references. I have included the text of the verses so you won't have to look them up yourself. Please read them. They are very important.

Each chapter is followed by a prayer that I wrote for *The NIV Worship Bible.* I hope you will pray these prayers with me. Let them become starting points for your own prayers—catalysts for your personal worship.

You will notice that I repeat myself quite a bit. That's deliberate. You will also find that I ask a lot of questions in this book. And that brings me back to my original question:

Are you looking for God?

Jesus said in John 4:23 that the Father is looking for worshipers. So if you are looking for God and you just can't seem to find him, then stop what you are doing and worship him—and he will come find you.[3]

Hear My Prayer

Sovereign Lord,
You are the Almighty Creator,
the Holy and Righteous One.
You are the Eternal Father,
the infinite Source of all life.
In Your presence are truth and wisdom.
Righteousness and justice surround Your throne.
I worship You, my God and Father,
with reverence and awe.
Please keep me close to Your side
so that I may hear Your voice,
learn Your ways and live a life
that is pleasing to You.
Amen.

SECTION ONE

Unexpected Mercy

Therefore, I urge you, brothers, in view of God's mercy...

TWO

A Defining Moment

God sent the Spirit of his Son into our hearts, the Spirit who calls out, "Abba, Father." So you are no longer a slave, but a son; and since you are a son, God has made you also an heir.

(Galatians 4:6-7)

"God isn't looking for servants. He is looking for sons and daughters who will join him in the family business." With those words I closed my message. I was addressing an audience of 1,500 pastors and worship leaders in Minneapolis. I was talking to them about their identity in Christ...not just *in* Christ, but in the eyes of Christ. I wanted them to take a closer look at how God looks at them.

When the meeting ended a man came to the altar. He had tears in his eyes. He said, "I have been a pastor for 25 years. I have spent my life trying to be a good and faithful servant. But my ministry has been a lifelong struggle to feel connected to God, to find some sense of fulfillment and belonging. Today I realized for the first time that my identity has been that of a servant; I have never been a son. God has been my Lord and master, but he hasn't been my Father. I need to be born again."

For 25 years, this hard-working man had diligently served the Lord out of a sense of duty, but never out of joy. He thought that by serving God he would earn God's blessing.

He was trying desperately to come into God's presence, but he was coming in through the back door—the servants' entrance. He had never come in through the front door—the family entrance. For him, coming to God was coming to work instead of coming home.

But service does not qualify us to come into God's presence—God's mercy does.

> But I, by your great mercy,
> will come into your house;
> in reverence will I bow down
> toward your holy temple.
> (Psalm 5:7)

The way of a worshiper begins with God's mercy. It is because of his mercy that God accepts our worship at all. What exactly does "mercy" mean? According to my bright red *Webster's New World Dictionary, Third College Edition,* here is the definition of "mercy":

> **Mercy:** a disposition or inclination to forgive and to be kind.

God in his mercy is predisposed to forgive us—in other words, forgiveness is his "default setting"—it is his natural inclination. And kindness is the lens through which God sees us—it is the context for all of his consideration of us. No other God loves sinners.

Who is a God like you,
 who pardons sin and forgives [our] transgression?
You do not stay angry forever
 but delight to show mercy. (Micah 7:18)

Because God by his nature is inclined to be kind to us, he invites us to offer ourselves to him in worship. But how do we do that? What does worship mean, anyway? Most folks tend to think of worship in terms of specific activities, such as singing or going to church. Or they might take a broader view of worship as a kind of obsession, the way a man might dote on his car or a teenager might idolize a rock star. But idol worship is simply a misdirection of our God-summoned energies and affections—a self-imposed limitation on our capacity for the eternal. After all, cars break down (and so do some rock stars, for that matter).

Authentic worship is a response to an authentic encounter with the living God.

Authentic worship is barging in on eternity.

Consider this definition:

Worship:[from the old English weorthscipe or worth-ship] to ascribe, assign, attribute, declare worth

When we worship God, we declare his worth. But in order to declare God's worth, we must first discover his worth. And that brings me to a question:

What is God worth to you?

To the extent that you can answer that question, you will be a worshiper. Your life will reflect his value, both in the things you say and, more convincingly, by the way you live. But you will also find that that question can never be fully answered. The discovery of God's worth is both endless and endlessly rewarding.

Our hunger for God is itself God-given. God is the Initiator. He is before everything else. He is a Father by his nature. He is seminal in his character. Everything we do for God is in response to what God has done for us. Everything we have comes from his hand. We live because God gives us life. We breathe because God gives us breath. We thrive because God gives us fruitfulness. We are holy because God gives us holiness.

Our acts of worship are responses to what God has already done. We praise him because he has revealed his glory to us. We give out of the bounty he has given to us. We repent, not to earn forgiveness, but because he has already offered forgiveness—Christ died for us while we were sinners. We serve him, not to become his children, but because we are his children—children who have joined him in the family business.

We worship God, not to win an audience with him, but because he first came seeking an audience with us. Worship doesn't drag God into our presence. God is always present. We are surrounded by his omnipresence, but we eagerly desire his manifest presence within us and among us.

God's manifest presence is the token of his friendship. God's friendship is the reward of worship.

So how do we discover God's worth? I believe that an understanding of God's worth begins with an understanding of our worth to God. After all, "We love him because he first loved us" (1Jn 4:19, NKJV). So let's look at ourselves through God's eyes.

Let's look at ourselves "in view of God's mercy."

Hear My Prayer

Our great, loving and merciful God,
I praise You for making Yourself known to us.
Yet even in Your disclosure You remain a mystery.
You cannot be contained,
yet You dwell in my heart.
You cannot be restrained,
yet You wait for me to follow.
You cannot be defined, yet You delight
in my words of worship.
You are more powerful
than all the forces of nature combined,
yet You choose to be moved by the prayer of a child.
You make all the rules,
yet You choose to love me without condition.
You are more than life itself.
You are what all of nature is trying to describe.
O wonderful, awesome God,
though now I see only a shadow of Your glory,
I know that one day I will see You face to face.
Amen.

THREE

The Seeker

I revealed myself to those who did not ask for me;
I was found by those who did not seek me. (Isaiah 65:1)

In Genesis chapter 3 we read some of the saddest and at the same time most hope-filled words in all of Scripture. Adam and Eve have just sinned. Mankind has fallen. Innocence is lost. For the first time, Adam and Eve feel fear. And they hide from God...

> Then the eyes of both of them were opened, and they realized they were naked; so they sewed fig leaves together and made coverings for themselves.
>
> Then the man and his wife heard the sound of the Lord God as he was walking in the garden in the cool of the day, and they hid from the Lord God among the trees of the garden. But the Lord God called to the man, "Where are you?"
>
> He answered, "I heard you in the garden, and I was afraid because I was naked; so I hid." (Genesis 3:7-10)

Adam and Eve hid from God. They did not look for him; but God in his mercy came looking for them. If God had not sought them out, if he had simply abandoned them and left them in their hiding place, they would never have found God. Matthew Henry says of Adam:

> *If God had not called to him, his condition would have been as desperate as that of fallen angels; this lost sheep would have wandered endlessly if the Good Shepherd had not sought after him to bring him back.*[1]

God is the Seeker. He is the one who initiates relationship. He doesn't turn his back on us. He comes looking for us in our failure and sin. He calls us out of our hiding places, not to condemn us, but to redeem us.

In the Gospel of Matthew, we find these two parables of Jesus that illustrate the immeasurable value God places on us:

> The kingdom of heaven is like treasure hidden in a field. When a man found it, he hid it again, and then in his joy went and sold all he had and bought that field.
>
> Again, the kingdom of heaven is like a merchant looking for fine pearls. When he found one pearl of great price, he went away and sold everything he had and bought it.
>
> (Matthew 13:44-46)

If you ask most Christians what these parables mean, they will reply that the kingdom of God is worth everything to them—that we should be willing to give up all our worldly possessions to follow Jesus. Though those statements are true, consider this question: Can you purchase the kingdom of God like the man bought the field or the merchant bought the pearl? Perhaps we have this backwards.

The first 43 verses of Matthew chapter 13 contain the Parable of the Sower, the Parable of the Weeds, and the Parable of the Mustard Seed. In each of these parables, the man is the Lord. So why is it when we come to the parables of the Hidden Treasure and the Pearl of Great Price, that we suddenly interpret the man and the merchant to be ourselves? Isn't it Jesus who, "though he was rich, yet for your sakes he became poor" (2Co 8:9)? Isn't it Jesus who, "being in very nature God, did not consider equality with God something to be grasped, but made himself nothing...and became obedient to death—even death on a cross," (Php 2:6-8) so that he might redeem us and bring us into his kingdom?

I think what Jesus is really saying in these parables is that the Lord is the "man," the world is the "field" and you are the "hidden treasure."

The Lord is the "merchant looking for fine pearls" and you are the "pearl of great price."

In the 15th chapter of Luke, Jesus tells two parables that reveal more of God's tenacious search for us.

> Then Jesus told them this parable: "Suppose one of you has a hundred sheep and loses one of them. Does he not leave the ninety-nine in the open country and go after the lost sheep until he finds it? And when he finds it, he joyfully puts it on his shoulders and goes home. Then he calls his friends and neighbors together and says, 'Rejoice with me; I have found my lost sheep.' I tell you that in the same way there will be more

rejoicing in heaven over one sinner who repents than over ninety-nine righteous persons who do not need to repent.

"Or suppose a woman has ten silver coins and loses one. Does she not light a lamp, sweep the house and search carefully until she finds it? And when she finds it, she calls her friends and neighbors together and says, 'Rejoice with me; I have found my lost coin.' In the same way, I tell you, there is rejoicing in the presence of the angels of God over one sinner who repents." (Luke 15:3-10)

I praise God for the incredible value he places on sinners! He does not passively wait for us to come to him. He actively, passionately seeks after us and calls us out of our wanderings and hiding places. His pursuit is relentless. Nine out of ten is not good enough for him. Ninety-nine out of one hundred is still unacceptable. He is not willing that any should perish. He wants all people "to be saved and to come to a knowledge of the truth" (1Ti 2:4). When he finds us he carries us on his shoulders into the safety of the fold. He rejoices with saints and angels.

God is the Seeker.

You are just what he is looking for.

You are his passion.

You are his treasure.

You are his most precious possession.

Hear My Prayer

Lord God, You have sought us in Your love,
You have pursued us with Your grace,
You have captured us by Your mercy in Jesus.
Your intention from the dawn of creation
was to be in relationship with us.
Why would You choose us? We hide. You seek.
We hold back. You pour Yourself out on our behalf.
We are weak, broken and unresponsive.
Yet You are relentless in Your pursuit of us.
You are determined to make us holy
and blameless in Your sight.
We will never fully comprehend
the depth of Your love or the riches
of Your grace in Christ Jesus.
All praise be to You, our loving Lord!
Amen.

FOUR

INNOCENCE FOUND

The Lord God made garments of skin for Adam and his wife and he clothed them. (Genesis 3:21)

Adam and Eve lost their innocence. They clothed themselves with fig leaves. But God removed the garments that Adam and Eve made for themselves and replaced them with garments he fashioned with his own hands—garments made of animal skin—garments that required the shedding of innocent blood, because "it is the blood that makes atonement for one's life," (Lev 17:11) and "without the shedding of blood there is no forgiveness" (Heb 9:22).

Here in the garden the groundwork was laid for God's plan of redemption: God pursued man; innocent blood was shed to cover guilt; God made a way to restore our relationship with him. Looking back upon this scene, the words of the Apostle Paul reveal the substance of these shadows:

When we were utterly helpless...God showed his great love for us by sending Christ to die for us while we were still sinners. (Romans 5:6,8, NLT)

How often do we try to hide from God when we fail? When sin strips us of our innocence, do we attempt to cover ourselves with fig leaves of self-righteousness? Do we really think we can hide from God?

You see, when God calls out to you, "Where are you?" it's not because he doesn't know the answer. God knows right where you are. He simply wants to make sure that you know the answer. He invites you to step out of your hiding place into the light of the sun, to let go of your self-righteousness so that he can clothe you in his righteousness. God isn't looking for perfection—he knows you're not perfect. But he's looking for honesty. He wants you to come out of hiding and admit to yourself what he already knows.

Through the shed blood of Jesus, "the Lamb of God, who takes away the sin of the world," (Jn 1:29) God takes away our "fig leaves" and clothes us with his garments of salvation.

> I delight greatly in the Lord;
> my soul rejoices in my God.
> For he has clothed me with garments of salvation
> and arrayed me in a robe of righteousness.
> (Isaiah 61:10)

> At one time we too were foolish, disobedient, deceived and enslaved by all kinds of passions and pleasures. We lived in malice and envy, being hated and hating one another. But when the kindness and love of God our Savior appeared, he saved us, not because of righteous things we had done, but because of his mercy. (Titus 3:3-5)

We think we cannot come to God because we are unclean. Or we think that there is no way that he can use us because we are such messed up people. So we stay away. We hide. We try to cover ourselves with good deeds. We think we have to do something to make ourselves holy and acceptable before we can come to God—to somehow prove our worthiness to him.

But holiness is not what God wants *from* you. Holiness is what God wants *for* you.

You cannot make yourself holy. Only God can make you holy. You cannot earn holiness—your generous acts of charity may make you a great philanthropist, but they will not make you holy. You cannot learn holiness—your wealth of Bible knowledge may make you a great theologian, but it will not make you holy. Holiness is God's gift of grace. The only way to get holiness is to surrender to it.

> I am the Lord, who makes you holy. (Exodus 31:13)
> I am the Lord, who makes you holy. (Leviticus 20:8)
> I am the Lord, who makes you holy. (Leviticus 22:32)

The prophet Isaiah says, "all our righteous acts are like filthy rags; we all shrivel up like a leaf" (Isa 64:6). God doesn't want our holiness—he wants his holiness in us. Our attempts at holiness are like Adam and Eve's fig leaves—poor substitutes for the real thing. Real holiness, God's holiness, requires the shedding of blood, and the blood of Jesus Christ has been shed so that we might be clothed in his righteousness. And so the writer of Hebrews says:

> Both the one who makes men holy and those who are made holy are of the same family. So Jesus is not ashamed to call them brothers. (Hebrews 2:11)

Hear those words again: "Both the one who makes men holy and those who are made holy are of the same family. So Jesus is not ashamed to call them brothers." If Jesus is our brother, then God is our Father. Again, in Hebrews chapter 11, the writer says that God is not ashamed to be called our God. Dear ones, hear the word of the Lord:

God is not ashamed of you. He loves you,
and he is proud to be your Father.

Oh yes, he hates sin. Sin separates us from God. But when we sin, we have a mediator, a covering, a Savior. He is Christ, the Lord.

Even now my witness is in heaven;
my advocate is on high.
My intercessor is my friend
as my eyes pour out tears to God;
on behalf of a man he pleads with God
as a man pleads for his friend. (Job 16:19-21)

For there is one God and one mediator between God and men, the man Christ Jesus, who gave himself as a ransom for all men. (1Timothy 2:5-6)

Therefore he is able to save completely those who come to God through him, because he always lives to intercede for them. (Hebrews 7:25)

But if anybody does sin, we have one who speaks to the Father in our defense—Jesus Christ, the Righteous One. (1 John 2:1)

Our advocate is the Lord Jesus Christ: commissioned by the Father, trusted by God to accomplish redemption for us, and trusted by us to perfect that which he has begun in us. What greater advocate could we have before God than the Friend of sinners who was sent by God himself to be a ransom for us? And so the songwriter says:

I need no other argument.
I need no other plea.
It is enough that Jesus died,
And that he died for me.
"My Faith Has Found a Resting Place"
Lidie Edmunds (1891)

The blood of Jesus purifies us from all sin and makes us holy (1Jn 1:7). Not just some sins, not just the little sins, but ALL sin. And both the one who makes us holy and we who are made holy are of the same family. So Jesus is not ashamed to call us brothers and sisters. I say it again:

God is not ashamed of you. He loves you,
and he is proud to be your Father.

He will never grow tired of you. He loves you with a love that will not weaken its hold. He loves you with a love that is more durable than life itself. He loves you with a love that is more tenacious, more jealous, more secure, and more devoted than the love of any earthly parent. Listen to the voice of the Father from Isaiah 49:

> Can a mother forget the baby at her breast
> and have no compassion on the child she has borne?
> Though she may forget,
> I will not forget you!
> See, I have engraved you on the palms of my hands...
> (Isaiah 49:15-16)

"I have engraved you on the palms of my hands." Do you understand what that means? You are God's tattoo! You are engraved on the palms of his hands. It means that you are never out of his sight or beyond his reach. What greater hope can there be than this? The hands that create, the hands that heal, the hands that defend and provide and comfort and correct—the very hands of God—have your name written on them.

The Father loves you with a love that cannot be bought or earned or traded or sold. His love will never let go or give up or ease off or break down. He longs for you, and calls to you, and woos you to his heart. And if he cannot entice you to himself through blessing, then he just might drive you to himself through adversity. He knows your struggles, your doubts, your fears, your disappointments, your questions. He doesn't always take the bad things away, but he will fill your experience with his presence.

He loves you so much that he gave his only begotten Son to die for you. If you will just believe in him, you will not perish, but have everlasting life. For God didn't send his Son into the world to condemn you, but that through him you might be saved and made holy, and restored to intimate relationship with your heavenly Father.

God is not ashamed of you. He loves you. And he bids you to come to him and unburden yourself of the weight of sin and guilt.

> Come to me, all you who are weary and burdened, and I will give you rest. Take my yoke upon you and learn from me, for I am gentle and humble in heart, and you will find rest for your souls. For my yoke is easy and my burden is light. (Matthew 11:28-30)

Some people say, "You don't know my past. You don't know my present. You don't know the trouble I'm in. You don't know the weight that I'm carrying." And you're right, I don't. But God does, and you do. And he wants you to come to him—to bring it to Jesus.

Some of you reading these words today carry the burden and the memory of a horrible past, and it has paralyzed you. You may have committed violent acts; you may be struggling with addictions and habits and thought patterns; you may be living with the guilt of abortion, or sexual sin...and you think, "There is just no way I can come to God—not in the condition I'm in. I'm too far gone. I've tried it before—too many times—and I've failed. That stuff may be good for other people, but it's too late for me."

If you think you are too sinful for God, then you are just what he is looking for. Jesus came to seek and to save the lost (Lk 19:10). You really can't come to grips with God's forgiveness until you are willing to admit how unworthy you are.

But listen, my friend. God is not asking you to make a promise that you cannot keep. He is inviting you to receive a promise that only he can keep:[1]

> If we confess our sins, he is faithful and just and will forgive us our sins and purify us from all unrighteousness. (1 John 1:9)

God already knows all of your failures. He knows your pain and your sorrow. He knows what you did last night. He knows what you will do tomorrow. There is nothing you can tell him that is going to surprise him. He longs for you to come to him, to talk with him about your sins, and to receive his forgiveness so that he can heal you.

We think our sin makes us worthless to God. But listen to what God has to say about us:

> For this is what the Lord says:
> "You were sold for nothing,
> and without money you will be redeemed." (Isaiah 52:3)

You see, once you were a slave to sin. You sold yourself out for nothing; but all the money in the world could not buy your freedom. So God redeemed you. He bought your freedom, not with money, but with his own blood.

Sin made you worthless; but to God, you are priceless.

Now God has decreed holiness for you—so surrender to it. The one who makes you holy and you who are made holy are of the same family. So Jesus is not ashamed to call you his sister or his brother.

God is not ashamed of you. He loves you.
And he is proud to be your Father.

Hear My Prayer

I am made complete in the One
who is completely God.
I am possessed and embraced by the One
in whose nature is fullness of life
and hope and peace.
In You, Christ Jesus, Holy One,
I am now holy.
In You, Christ Jesus, Peace Maker,
I am now reconciled to God.
In You, Christ Jesus, Mystery of God,
I am now hidden.
Only in You is found
this truth beyond imagination,
this love beyond reason,
this grace beyond measure:
God is not ashamed of me!
What rest, what joy,
what unspeakable wonder is mine
to know that because I am in You, Lord Jesus,
God is proud to call Himself my Father.
Amen.

FIVE

The Prodigal Father

How great is the love the Father has lavished on us, that we should be called children of God! And that is what we are!

(1 John 3:1)

Some people may take offense at my assertion that God is "proud" to be your Father. By pride I don't mean haughtiness or arrogance. What I mean is that God takes great delight in you, like a father delighting in his newborn child. Perhaps a personal story can best illustrate the pride of our heavenly Father.

In the year 2000, I attended a Promise Keepers conference in Denver, Colorado. On Friday evening, at the downbeat of the opening worship time, I stepped out from the backstage production area to see how the men in the arena were engaging in worship.

Seated in the front row was a man in his early fifties. His teenaged son was seated next to him in a wheel chair. It was dreadfully obvious at first glance that this boy was severely handicapped. I learned later that he had suffered a spinal cord injury playing high school football. The boy was paralyzed from the neck down. He was blind and unable to speak.

When the music started, I witnessed the most remarkable living demonstration of the Father's love that I have ever seen. As 16,000 men stood to sing "All Hail the Power of Jesus Name," this father turned and faced his son. He slipped his hands beneath the boy's arms, lifted him out of his wheelchair, and held him in a bear hug. There they stood, face-to-face, not more than six inches apart from one another. The father began singing to his son.

The boy couldn't see his father's face, but he could feel his touch and hear his voice. Slowly, a smile came to the boy's face, like a sunrise breaking through a clouded horizon. The boy was able, with great exertion, to wrap his right arm around his father's neck. And for the next ten minutes they stood in one another's arms, a proud, loving father singing to his crippled son.

The father's face was full of love and pride for his son, not because of anything the boy could do, but simply because of who the boy was—the father's son—broken, helpless, but beautiful in his father's eyes. As I watched in tearful amazement, I remembered these cherished words from Scripture:

> The Lord your God is with you,
>   he is mighty to save.
> He will take great delight in you,
>   he will quiet you with his love,
>   he will rejoice over you with singing.
> (Zephaniah 3:17)

What I saw that night was the Word in flesh, dwelling among us. I saw a father taking great delight in his son, quieting him with his love and rejoicing over him with singing—grace embracing brokenness; joy triumphing over tragedy. In this father's eyes, I saw the love and pride of my heavenly Father. In the son, I saw myself and millions of other broken, helpless people.

Like this man, our heavenly Father loves us. Not because of what we can do for him, but because of who we are—his sons and daughters, in whom he takes great delight. And he rejoices over us with singing. And so I say:

God is not ashamed of you. He loves you,
and he is proud to be your Father.

Another story comes to mind. It is the third parable that Jesus told in Luke chapter 15. It is the Parable of the Lost Son, more commonly referred to as "The Prodigal Son."

> There was a man who had two sons. The younger one said to his father, "Father, give me my share of the estate." So he divided his property between them.
>
> Not long after that, the younger son got together all he had, set off for a distant country and there squandered his wealth in wild living. After he had spent everything, there was a severe famine in that whole country, and he began to be in need. So he went and hired himself out to a citizen of that country, who sent him to his fields to feed pigs.
>
> He longed to fill his stomach with the pods that the pigs were eating, but no one gave him anything.
>
> When he came to his senses, he said, "How many of my father's hired men have food to spare, and here I am starving to death! I will set out and go back to my father and say to him:

> Father, I have sinned against heaven and against you. I am no longer worthy to be called your son; make me like one of your hired men." So he got up and went to his father.
>
> But while he was still a long way off, his father saw him and was filled with compassion for him; he ran to his son, threw his arms around him and kissed him.
>
> The son said to him, "Father, I have sinned against heaven and against you. I am no longer worthy to be called your son."
>
> But the father said to his servants, "Quick! Bring the best robe and put it on him. Put a ring on his finger and sandals on his feet. Bring the fattened calf and kill it. Let's have a feast and celebrate. For this son of mine was dead and is alive again; he was lost and is found." So they began to celebrate. (Luke 15:11-24)

Read the story again. Nowhere in the text, in any translation for that matter, is the boy called a "prodigal son." I have found there to be a common misunderstanding of the word "prodigal." Most people think that prodigal means wayward or rebellious. But that is not what it means. Again, according to my bright red *Webster's New World Dictionary, Third College Edition,* here is the definition of "prodigal":

> **prodigal:** 1) exceedingly or recklessly wasteful; 2) extremely generous; lavish; 3) extremely abundant; profuse.

With this definition in mind, read the story a third time. Who is the real prodigal in the story? The boy is not the prodigal. Granted, the boy is wasteful with his resources. But perhaps he is more like his father than we realize at first glimpse. The father is exceedingly, recklessly "wasteful" with his love. The father extremely, abundantly, profusely lavishes his love on this undeserving boy.

The father is the prodigal.

And so is our Father.

Regardless of our failure and rebellion, our Father lavishes his love on us. We, like the son, come to our senses and decide to return to our Father, broken, empty-handed, ashamed. While we are still a long way off, our Father sees us and is filled with compassion for us. He runs to us, throws his arms around us and kisses us. We tell him we are not worthy to be called his children. But our prodigal Father says, "Nonsense! You are my son, my daughter. You were dead, but now you are alive again. You were lost, but now you are found." And then the celebration begins.

God is not ashamed of you. He loves you,
and he is proud to be your Father.

If only I could tell you how much God loves you. How passionate he is for you. How deeply he cares about you. He has always been after you, calling you, wooing you, waiting for you to come to him.

Love is not simply God's choice—love is his nature. He loves you with a perfect love—an everlasting love—a relentless love—an unquenchable, insatiable, immeasurable, inexhaustible, irrepressible, irrational, inescapable love. There is nothing you can do to make him love you more. And there is absolutely nothing you can do to make him love you less. He doesn't love you for what you do; he loves you for who you are—his son, his daughter, his lost one, his found one. He loves you. And he wants a deep, abiding relationship with you. He longs to fill your life with himself.

The Apostle Paul wrote:

> And I pray that you, being rooted and established in love, may have power, together with all the saints, to grasp how wide and long and high and deep is the love of Christ, and to know this love that surpasses knowledge. (Ephesians 3:17-19)

"...how wide and long and high and deep...this love that surpasses knowledge..." How can we understand that which is beyond explanation? How can we measure the immeasurable? How can we know that which surpasses knowledge? After all the evil we have done to our Lord Jesus, who of us would even dare to ask for his love? It would be unthinkable. Yet we are contained within its boundaries, upheld and sustained within its width and length and height and depth. We will never find the outermost limits of his love for us.

The Psalmist wrote:

> Where can I go from your Spirit?
> Where can I flee from your presence?
> If I go up to the heavens, you are there;
> if I make my bed in the depths, you are there.

If I rise on the wings of the dawn,
if I settle on the far side of the sea,
even there your hand will guide me,
your right hand will hold me fast.
(Psalm 139:7-10)

I don't know how to say it adequately or accurately enough—words simply cannot express the love God has for you. There are 783,134 words (give or take a jot or tittle) in the King James Bible, and they still fall short of expressing the fullness of the love of God. How many more words will it take to tell of his love for you?

As the songwriter wrote:

Could we with ink the ocean fill,
And were the skies of parchment made,
Were every stalk on earth a quill,
And every man a scribe by trade,
To write the love of God above
Would drain the ocean dry.
Nor could the scroll contain the whole,
Though stretched from sky to sky.
"The Love of God"
Frederick Lehman (1917)

So what does all this have to do with worship? As I said before, I believe that understanding God's worth to us begins with an understanding of our worth to God. We love him because he first loved us (1Jn 4:19, NKJV). We come to him because he first called out to us. We live for him because he sent his son to die for us.

God is the Initiator. If he did not first love us and call us and reveal himself to us, we could never hope to know him. But once we begin to glimpse his immeasurable love for us, we find stirring within us a deep desire to respond with love and gratitude.

We know what we are worth to God. We are worth the life of his Son. The Father sent Jesus into the world to redeem us and restore us to fellowship with God so that we might worship him. Our worship is worth infinitely more to God than the worship of the rest of creation. Human beings are the only ones who worship God from redeemed hearts. God didn't take on the form of animals; he took on the form of man and became one of us. Jesus didn't die to save cats or dogs or birds or whales; he didn't die to save fallen angels or any other creatures. He died to save mankind and restore us to God. We are the only ones that Jesus died for.

So we know what we are worth to our Prodigal Father.[1]

The question is: What is our Father worth to you?

Hear My Prayer

Lord, teach me the right way
to live in freedom—
not freedom to live in whatever
manner I choose
but freedom to live the way
You have always wanted me to live.
You have set me free from sin;
now teach me to flee from sin.
Teach me to walk in the new way of the Spirit.
May I never bring shame or
disgrace to the name of Jesus;
rather, may I point the way
for others to meet You and
receive Your gift of grace as well.
Amen.

SIX

The Untold Riches of Worship

He who dwells in the secret place of the Most High
shall abide under the shadow of the Almighty.
I will say of the Lord, "He is my refuge and my fortress;
my God, in him I will trust." (Psalm 91:1, NKJV)

When I was a kid, my favorite game was Hide 'n Seek. There was nothing more fun than hunkering down in a great hiding place and trying to outsmart "It." On warm summer nights all the kids on the block would gather in front of Tadd Floyd's house and disturb the peace till way past curfew: stomping through flower beds, pestering the neighbors' dogs, hurdling split-rail fences—ducking, weaving, peeking, sneaking, running for "home" as fast as our PF Flyers could get us there. We looked like little ghosts scampering from house to house. Oh, the stealth of it all. It was the height of intrigue for a nine-year-old boy. And I was a master of the game. My face could have been on the Wheaties' box for Hide 'n Seek.

As a champion Hide 'n Seek player, I can tell you that a great hiding place has two requirements: it has to be dark and it has to be confined. Under normal circumstances, such a place would be frightening to a child. But in the excitement of the hunt, it is a refuge.

What does this have to do with worship? You'll see in a minute...

◆

In the book of Isaiah we read of a vision the prophet had of the throne of God.

> I saw the Lord seated on a throne, high and exalted, and the train of his robe filled the temple. (Isaiah 6:1)

Let's think about that picture for a moment. God is seated on a throne. The train, or hem, of his robe fills the temple, the place of worship. Where, then, is the throne in relationship to the temple? The throne is placed above the temple.

In Psalm 22:3 David tells us that the Lord is enthroned on the praises of his people. In other words, the throne of God rests on our praises. Does that mean that if we do not praise him there will be no place for his throne? Not exactly; rather, it means that when we praise him we come under his throne and bring ourselves into alignment with his authority. We come into his presence when we worship him.

Matthew Henry wrote:

> *It is a throne of glory, before which we must worship—*
> *a throne of government, under which we must be subject*
> *—a throne of grace, to which we may come boldly.*[1]

It is this third aspect, the throne of grace, on which I want to focus.

James 4:6 tells us that God resists the proud but gives grace to the humble. Here is another way of saying it: Pride is a repellent of grace. But humility attracts the grace of God.

Worship is an act of humility. It is impossible to truly worship and be proud at the same time, because worship is a declaration of dependence—it is an honest admission that God is greater than I am. A proud man praises no one. As C. S. Lewis said, "A proud man is always looking down on things and people: and, of course, as long as you are looking down, you cannot see something that is above you."[2] But a humble man will recognize and declare the worth of others.

Hebrews 4:16(NKJV) tells us, "Come boldly to the throne of grace, that we may obtain mercy and find grace to help in time of need." How can we come humbly and boldly at the same time? Aren't humility and boldness opposed to each other? It's important to remember that we approach a throne of grace, not judgment. So we come humbly and boldly: humbly because we know we do not deserve God's mercy; boldly because we need not fear his wrath. To come humbly does not mean to grovel. To come boldly does not mean to come disrespectfully. To come humbly is to come without pride or pretense. To come boldly is to come without fear or doubting. We come humbly because we know we have no right to be there on our own. We come boldly because we've been invited by the King himself. No one can turn us away.

When we come to God in humility and worship him boldly, we submit ourselves to him and surrender to his sovereignty. By doing this we make ourselves available to the outpouring of God's grace. But if we stubbornly refuse to praise him, if we stand firm in our pride, then we will be out of alignment with his throne. We will have removed ourselves from the flow of his gracious provision.

Am I saying that we somehow earn God's grace by flattering him with our words? No. But I am saying that worship brings us into a deeper dimension of spiritual well-being. We are much more likely to live in the King's favor when we live at the King's feet. Or to put it another way, we are more likely to get wet by standing in the river than by wandering in the desert. To come humbly and boldly to the throne of God is to stand in the river of his grace.

Worship is not some kind of magic key to worldly wealth. Rather, worship unlocks the door to the treasures of heaven—treasures that cannot be measured: unfailing love, peace that transcends all understanding, wisdom beyond our natural abilities, strength for today, hope for tomorrow, daily bread, forgiveness of sins, kindness that leads us to repentance, mercy that triumphs over judgment, an eternal inheritance that can never perish, spoil or fade—these are the untold riches that await us at the throne of grace. They are ours for the taking. But we have to come and get them.

◆

Now let's get back to the Hide 'n Seek story.

Twenty-five years later.

For most young men, their sense of worth is wrapped up in their work. I was like most young men—consumed with my career, a bit arrogant, dreaming of greatness...and dangerously close to burnout. I was stunned by my own fragility.

One day, after four years on the job at Maranatha! Music, a new boss came to the office. He asked tough questions. He challenged old ways of thinking. He gave me the once-over—more than once. And I came up short. I was given time to think about what I really wanted to do with my life. At that point, I had no idea how patient and honorable he was. I felt misunderstood, unappreciated, marginalized. I didn't want to leave, but I didn't see how I could stay. And I desperately wanted to stay. I was quite distraught. I was a young husband and father facing an uncertain future.

I found myself in a dark, confined space. And I feared it. Even in broad daylight, there seemed to be a pall over my life. I felt small and unnecessary.

The Prophet Nahum wrote:

> His way is in the whirlwind and the storm,
> and clouds are the dust of his feet. (Nahum 1:3)

There definitely were clouds looming overhead. But I believed that God was in them, leading the way through the storm. Day after day I surrendered to God's sovereignty, and followed him deeper into it all. I cried out to him in prayer and worship. I didn't want to ask God, "Why are you doing this to me?" Instead, I asked, "What lesson do you want me to learn?"

I searched the Scriptures.

I searched my heart.

I watched.

I listened.

Heaven was silent. But I kept myself at the foot of the throne. I was determined to get in God's way.

Sometimes praise defies reason. But someone once said, "The heart knows reasons that reason never knows." Even when it didn't make sense, I knew in my heart that I needed to offer sacrifices of praise and thanksgiving to God. So I set my heart in a posture of praise.

I turned my car into a sanctuary by turning off the radio and devoting my drive time to prayer and worship. Sometimes I drove the long way home just so I could spend more time talking to God.

Weeks passed.

The darkness persisted. The anxiety deepened. The heaviness intensified. I didn't know how long I could go on. I prayed. And prayed. "Father, if I stand, may I stand in your strength. If I fall, may I fall into your grace. Do whatever it takes for as long as it takes, Lord. Just don't let me miss the lesson, because I don't want to have to go through this again."

What was this darkness? What was this pressure? Why did I feel trapped? Everything seemed so—I don't know how else to describe it—thick.

On September 22, 1992, I was awakened at 4:00am with this question in my mind: "When did you learn to fear a hiding place?" I sat straight up in bed and listened to the question again: "When did you learn to fear a hiding place?" I got out of bed and stumbled to the kitchen table. As I waited in listening prayer, I remembered the joy of my childhood game and my love for hiding places.

Then I heard these words whispered deep within my heart:

"The darkness is a fold in my cloak.
The pressure is my hand holding you close to my side.
I am hiding you."

As I sat at the table thanking God for his kindness, my fears began to abate. The heaviness lifted. I was so keenly aware of the presence of God in my life, watching over me, protecting me, hiding me.

God knew. He really knew. And he was intimately involved in the struggle.

I can't say there was nothing to fear—oh, there was still plenty to fear. My troubles didn't go away right then and there. The darkness didn't suddenly turn to light. But I was no longer afraid. I felt safe. I realized that my sacrifices of praise had met with God's pleasure. He was enthroned on my praises.

I had tapped into the untold riches of worship: peace that surpassed understanding, strength to face another day, confidence that my family would be provided for, hope for a future, joy in spite of the crisis—grace upon grace upon grace.

Like a hen covering her chicks with her wing, my Father was hiding me in the fold of his cloak. The darkness was no longer a place of fear. It was now a place of rest. I went back to bed and slept in peace.

That early autumn morning I came to a deeper understanding of Isaiah's words:

> I will give you treasures hidden in the darkness, secret riches;
> and you will know that I am doing this—
> I, the Lord, the God of Israel,
> the one who calls you by your name. (Isaiah 45:3, TLB)

Well, I never left Maranatha. Looking back, I can honestly say that I needed a good once-over. As the Apostle Paul said, "My conscience is clear, but that does not make me innocent" (1Co 4:4). The question wasn't, "Is Buddy doing things wrong?" Rather, the question was, "Is Buddy doing the right thing—is he in the right place?" I can see now that I was the one who misunderstood; I was the one who lacked appreciation.

In December of that year, Maranatha received a phone call from Promise Keepers asking us to provide worship for 52,000 men at a conference in Boulder, Colorado. Tom, the "new boss," asked me to handle it.

Today I'm in the right place, doing the right thing. And Tom is one of my dearest friends. We have been in ministry together for over a decade at Maranatha. We have shared the awesome privilege of directing the worship experience for over 4 million men through our ministry partnership with Promise Keepers. Tom is a great man of God, a wise leader, and probably the most trusting, generous person I have ever known. I see now that he wasn't trying to hurt me; he was trying to help me.

And I'm very, very grateful.

Hear My Prayer

Father, in Your hand are the
untold riches of heaven and earth.
In Your hand is the life of every creature
and the breath of all mankind.
In Your hand are strength and power
to exalt and give strength to all.
In Your hand are my life, my times
and all my ways.
All blessing, all provision, all protection,
all comfort, all joy, all peace,
all righteousness are in Your hand.
O let me stay hidden in Your hand, Father,
and I will lack nothing.
Amen.

SEVEN

The Gateway to Worship

God has two dwellings: one in heaven, and the other in a meek and thankful heart.

Izaak Walton (1593-1683)[1]

How do you become a worshiper? Where is the starting point? Worship begins with saying, "Thank you."

Psalm 100:4 says, "Enter his gates with thanksgiving..." In other words, gratitude is the gateway to worship. We enter the gates with thanksgiving, then we cross the courts with praise. Hebrews 12:28 says, "Be thankful, and so worship God acceptably." It all starts with saying thanks.

"Thank you." Two simple words that can be, at times, oh so difficult to say. Thankfulness is a discipline. It is a learned behavior. We have to teach our kids to say thank you, even when they are given something they don't necessarily want. And we have to remind ourselves to say thank you, too.

Giving thanks is a way for us to declare the glory of God. It keeps us in a heart-posture of surrender and humility. It reminds us that our lives are in someone else's hands. Thankfulness helps us recall God's wonderful acts of mercy and grace, and to recognize that these very acts are born out of his unchanging nature.

God's actions are demonstrations of his character. He does what he does because of who he is. He saves because he is the

Savior. He creates because he is the Creator. He heals because he is the Healer. He provides because he is the Provider. He comforts because he is the Comforter. As we thank God for what he does, we soon begin to worship God for who he is.

There are 137 verses of Scripture about offering thanks to God. Thankfulness is important to him. It should be important to us. Even the worship of heaven as described by John in Revelation includes expressions of thanksgiving:

> And the twenty-four elders, who were seated on their thrones before God, fell on their faces and worshiped God, saying:
> "We give thanks to you, Lord God Almighty,
> the One who is and who was,
> because you have taken your great power
> and have begun to reign." (Revelation 11:16)

If the worship in heaven includes thanksgiving, so should the worship on earth.

So here is a question that I must prayerfully ask myself everyday: Am I thankful? Is my heart full of gratitude or resentment? Gratitude and resentment cannot co-exist. Resentment is indignation toward God. It takes offense at apparent mistreatment. Resentment is the attitude that I did not get what I deserve—that I have somehow been unfairly injured or mistreated.

Resentment is rooted in pride;
it is watered with tears of self-pity;
it bears the fruit of bitterness;
and it scatters seeds of envy.

The resentful heart cannot say thank you for what it has been given, because it can only look at what it does not have. And therefore, the resentful heart cannot be a place of worship, because thanksgiving is the beginning of worship (Ps 100:4). In order to be a worshiper, I must learn to say thank you. Even in the hard times.

Especially in the hard times.

One of my favorite hymn lyrics was written in 1854 by a man named George Croly. I think of these words when I feel that I've earned the right to be resentful:

Spirit of God, descend upon my heart;
Wean it from earth, through all its pulses move;
Stoop to my weakness, mighty as Thou art,
And make me love Thee as I ought to love.

Teach me to feel that Thou art always nigh;
Teach me the struggles of the soul to bear,
To check the rising doubt, the rebel sigh;
Teach me the patience of unanswered prayer.
"Spirit of God, Descend Upon My Heart"
George Croly (1854)

If I have truly surrendered my life to God, then who am I to say anything but thank you for what comes to me from the Father's hand? As Job said, "Shall we accept good from God, and not trouble?" (Job 2:10). I have walked with the Lord long enough to know that many things I call "trouble" turn out for my good, and many things I perceived to be "good" have proven otherwise. If we truly believe that "In all things God works for the good of those who love him" (Ro 8:28), then we can say thank you in every joy or sorrow, every success or failure, every gain or loss. It isn't always easy. Sometimes it really is a sacrifice. But it is necessary.

The prophet Jonah, from inside the belly of the fish, said:

> But I, with a song of thanksgiving,
> will sacrifice to you.
> What I have vowed I will make good.
> Salvation comes from the Lord. (Jonah 2:9)

Jonah's sacrifice in the midst of his trial was a simple song of thanksgiving. He said thank you before he was set free. But it was not until Jonah said thank you that God brought about his deliverance.

The Apostle Paul wrote, "Give thanks in all circumstances, for this is God's will for you in Christ Jesus" (1Th 5:18). God's will is that we give thanks in all circumstances. In his letter to the Colossians, Paul wrote:

> Let the word of Christ dwell in you richly as you teach and admonish one another with all wisdom, and as you sing psalms, hymns and spiritual songs with gratitude in your hearts to God. And whatever you do, whether in word or deed, do it all in the name of the Lord Jesus, giving thanks to God the Father through him. (Colossians 3:16-17)

Surely there is something you can be thankful for today—your family, your friends, your home, just the fact that you are alive. Maybe you're grateful that today isn't as bad as yesterday was. Maybe you're grateful that tomorrow isn't here yet. You can be grateful for something. And yet, how much do we take for granted?

In the Gospel of Luke we read of an encounter Jesus had with ten lepers. It is a study in human nature and gratitude.

> As he was going into a village, ten men who had leprosy met him. They stood at a distance and called out in a loud voice, "Jesus, Master, have pity on us!"
>
> When he saw them, he said, "Go, show yourselves to the priests." And as they went, they were cleansed.
>
> One of them, when he saw he was healed, came back, praising God in a loud voice. He threw himself at Jesus' feet and thanked him—and he was a Samaritan.
>
> Jesus asked, "Were not all ten cleansed? Where are the other nine? Was no one found to return and give praise to God except this foreigner?" Then he said to him, "Rise and go; your faith has made you well." (Luke 17:12-19)

In the ancient world, leprosy was a terminal disease.

First it killed the soul.

Then it killed the body.

Leprosy carried the stigma of moral failure. The presence of the disease was perceived as evidence of sin. Its victims were sent to priests, not to doctors. They were pronounced "unclean" rather than "unhealthy"—sounds more like a verdict than a diagnosis. Lepers had to announce their presence in public with the cry "Unclean! Unclean!" The cry meant that they were not just unclean in body; it was a public confession that they were unclean through and through. Lepers could be beaten or whipped for appearing in public, and were often chased away with stones. No one dared touch a leper, because to touch a leper was to become unclean oneself.

Leprosy was a living death sentence that carried with it complete banishment from the presence of God and his people—a banishment that was prescribed by divine law:

> The person with such an infectious disease must wear torn clothes, let his hair be unkempt, cover the lower part of his face and cry out, "Unclean! Unclean!" As long as he has the infection he remains unclean. He must live alone; he must live outside the camp. (Leviticus 13:45-46)

To be a leper was to be rejected by God himself.

Put yourself in the sandals of a leper. Imagine living in such hopelessness. There is no one to love you. No one to caress you or hold your hand. No one to dry your tears or bind your wounds. No one, that is, except other lepers—people just like you—social outcasts, heaven's rejects, hell's hostages. No one can heal you but God, and he has abandoned you. Or so they say.

But Jesus in his mercy makes you well. To be cleansed of the disease is to be cleansed of the cause. Healing means forgiveness. Clean skin equals a clean heart.

How will you respond? Will you throw yourself at Jesus' feet and thank him? Or will you be so wrapped up with the gift that you forget the Giver? Apparently, there is a 90% chance that you will forget to say thank you.

If it is within our human nature to be ungrateful for God's greatest gifts, is there any question but that we fail to say thanks for his daily acts of kindness? For food and clothing, for friends and family, for the beauty of creation, for forgiveness and salvation, for the gift of his presence in our hearts?

Ten men called out to Jesus. Ten men were healed. Ten men were given a second chance at life. Ten men were once again acceptable to God and to his people. Ten men could finally go home.

One of them said thank you—and he was a Samaritan, the least likely of the bunch.

Did it matter to Jesus? Yes. He asked, "Where are the other nine?"

I think it still matters to Jesus.

Worship begins with two simple words: *Thank you.*

Hear My Prayer

Thank You, Lord, for Your great faithfulness.
You know what is best for me.
All of my sufficiency is in You.
You are my source and my sustenance.
You supply bread for my daily needs,
forgiveness for my daily sins
and strength for my daily burdens.
Help me in every circumstance to be fully content
with that which issues from Your gracious hand.
"Better the little that the righteous have
than the wealth of many wicked;
for the power of the wicked will be broken,
but the Lord upholds the righteous."
Amen.

SECTION TWO

A New Way of Living

Offer your bodies as
living sacrifices, holy and
pleasing to God—this is
your spiritual act of worship.
Do not conform any longer
to the pattern of this world,
but be transformed by the
renewing of your mind.

EIGHT

THE CHOICE

Those who cling to worthless idols
forfeit the grace that could be theirs. (Jonah 2:8)

Why does God want your body? Why does he want your worship?

Everyone worships something. It is inevitable. It's in our spiritual DNA. We were designed to worship. We were created to be temples.

Some people worship power. Some worship money. Some worship possessions. Some worship themselves. And some people worship the true and living God.

Jonah's words bear repeating—read them again slowly, aloud: "Those who cling to worthless idols forfeit the grace that could be theirs." This verse leads to a soul-searching question:

What worthless idols am I still clinging to
that are causing me to forfeit something
of the fullness of God's grace in my life?

There are several Old Testament Scriptures that give us a picture of this principle in action. Here are a couple to consider:

They rejected his decrees and the covenant he had made with their fathers and the warnings he had given them. They followed worthless idols and themselves became worthless.

They imitated the nations around them although the Lord had ordered them, "Do not do as they do," and they did the things the Lord had forbidden them to do. (2Kings 17:15)

This is what the Lord says:

"What fault did your fathers find in me,
that they strayed so far from me?
They followed worthless idols
and became worthless themselves."

(Jeremiah 2:5)

Our character is shaped by the things we worship. People who worship money become greedy. Those who worship power become ruthless. Men who worship women become lustful. People who worship themselves become arrogant.

But those who worship the true and living God become Christ-like.

And we, who with unveiled faces all reflect the Lord's glory, are being transformed into his likeness with ever-increasing glory, which comes from the Lord, who is the Spirit. (2Corinthians 3:18)

Romans 1:18-32 gives us a frightening picture of what happens to a person who refuses to worship God.

The wrath of God is being revealed from heaven against all the godlessness and wickedness of men who suppress the truth by their wickedness, since what may be known about God is plain to them, because God has made it plain to them. For since the creation of the world God's invisible qualities—his eternal power and divine nature—have been clearly seen, being understood from what has been made, so that men are without excuse.

For although they knew God, they neither glorified him as God nor gave thanks to him, but their thinking became futile and their foolish hearts were darkened. Although they claimed to be wise, they became fools and exchanged the glory of the immortal God for images made to look like mortal man and birds and animals and reptiles.

Therefore God gave them over in the sinful desires of their hearts to sexual impurity for the degrading of their bodies with one another. They exchanged the truth of God for a lie, and worshiped and served created things rather than the Creator—who is forever praised. Amen.

Because of this, God gave them over to shameful lusts. Even their women exchanged natural relations for unnatural ones. In the same way the men also abandoned natural relations with women and were inflamed with lust for one another. Men committed indecent acts with other men, and received in themselves the due penalty for their perversion.

Furthermore, since they did not think it worthwhile to retain the knowledge of God, he gave them over to a depraved mind, to do what ought not to be done. They have become filled with every kind of wickedness, evil, greed and depravity. They are full of envy, murder, strife, deceit and malice. They are gossips, slanderers, God-haters, insolent, arrogant and boastful; they invent ways of doing evil; they disobey their parents; they are senseless, faithless, heartless, ruthless. Although they know God's righteous decree that those who do such things deserve death, they not only continue to do these very things but also approve of those who practice them. (Romans 1:18-32)

Verse 21 says, "For although they knew God, they neither glorified him as God nor gave thanks to him." In other words, they knew God, but they would not worship him. The result follows in the next few verses:

- Their thinking became futile (v 21);
- Their foolish hearts were darkened (v21);
- God gave them over to sexual impurity (v24) (read those words again they are packed with danger—"God gave them over..."));
- God gave them over to shameful lusts (v26);
- God gave them over to a depraved mind (v28).

And then Paul gives us a laundry list of wickedness—issues that sound all too familiar: gossip, arrogance, envy, faithlessness, to name a few.

If you follow this trail of sin and failure back up the page to its source—from the depraved mind to shameful lusts to sexual impurity to a darkened heart to futile thinking—it leads to a fork in the road at verse 21.

The fork is a place of decision: they knew God, but they chose to not give him glory or thanks. And because of that choice, all of those other things happened.

As Jeremiah said, they worshiped worthless idols and so became worthless themselves (Jer 2:5).

We all stand at the same fork in the road. Which way will we go? Who will we worship? Will we glorify God and give him thanks? Or will we worship ourselves or some other created thing and march defiantly down the road to self-destruction?

The other road that we meet at the fork is described in Romans 12:1-2. Between Romans chapter 1 and Romans chapter 12, Paul tells us about the incredible mercy and love of God that he demonstrated for us in this:

> While we were still sinners, Christ died for us. (Romans 5:8)

So when we come to Romans chapter 12, Paul says:

> Therefore, I urge you, brothers, in view of God's mercy, to offer your bodies as living sacrifices, holy and pleasing to God—this is your spiritual act of worship. Do not conform any longer to the pattern of this world but be transformed by the renewing of your mind. Then you will be able to test and approve what God's will is—his good, pleasing and perfect will.
> (Romans 12:1-2)

Let's look at Paul's words for a moment and make an important distinction. Paul says, "don't conform any longer to the pattern of this world." The pattern of this world was in Romans chapter 1. According to the dictionary, to conform means to "make or become the same" or "to behave in a conventional way by accepting without question the customs, traditions and prevailing opinions of others." Paul goes on to say, "Be transformed by the renewing of your mind." To transform means to "change the condition, function, nature, character or personality" of something.

Conforming has to do with behavior. Transforming has to do with character.

We are conformers. God is the Transformer.

Conforming is something we do to ourselves by trying to fit in or to become like everyone else. *Transforming* is something God does to us. And he transforms us by renewing our minds. You see, God doesn't just want to change our behavior. He wants to change the way we think.

When we stop conforming to the pattern of this world, God begins transforming us to the pattern of his will.

So we have a choice. We can cling to worthless idols and refuse to worship God, and then spend the rest of our lives wrestling with the sins and failures of Romans 1. Or we can fall on God's mercy, present ourselves to him in worship, have our minds renewed from their futile thinking, and discover his will for us.

It's our choice.

And it's a choice we face everyday.

What will you choose today—to conform or to be transformed?

HEAR MY PRAYER

Almighty God, I pray for myself and
for Your church throughout the world.
As we continue to press on into the fullness
of life in Your kingdom,
let us give no place to the devil,
leave no room for sin,
give no thought to temptation,
make no compromise with unrighteousness,
strike no deal with the world,
defend no guilt of our own,
retain no memory of wickedness,
preserve no relic of idolatry,
loosen no standard of morality,
tolerate no alternative to holiness.
Help us, rather, to prepare our minds for action;
to be self-controlled;
to set our hope fully on the grace to be
given us when Jesus Christ is revealed.
As obedient children, let us not conform to the
evil desires we had when we lived in ignorance.
But just as You who called us are holy,
so may we be holy in all we do;
for it is written, "Be holy, because I am holy."
Amen.

NINE

THE PLACE OF HIS PRESENCE

For this is what the high and lofty One says –
he who lives forever, whose name is holy:
"I live in a high and holy place,
but also with him who is contrite and lowly in spirit,
to revive the spirit of the lowly
and to revive the heart of the contrite." (Isaiah 57:15)

In Romans 12:1 the Apostle Paul tells us, "offer your bodies as living sacrifices." He goes on to tell us that this is a "spiritual act of worship." We need to think about that statement for a minute. Offering our bodies is a spiritual act—it is a physical demonstration of a spiritual reality.

(Of course, the problem with a living sacrifice is that it keeps trying to crawl off the altar.)

But why are we told to offer our bodies to God? How is this a "spiritual act of worship"? Why doesn't Paul just say "Turn your heart to the Lord," or "Have nice thoughts about God"? Why does God want our bodies? I believe Paul answers that question in 1 Corinthians when he says:

Do you not know that your body is the temple of the Holy Spirit, who is in you, whom you have received from God? You are not your own; you were bought at a price. Therefore, honor God with your body. (1Corinthians 6:19-20)

Your body, your flesh and blood and bones, this "piece of earth," as it were, is the temple of the Holy Spirit. Your body, my body, the body of every redeemed, blood-bought person, is God's dwelling place.

Your body is God's house.

I can just imagine that if you had been looking over God's shoulder as he formed Adam from the dust of the ground and if you could have asked him, "What are you making?" he would have said, "I'm building a temple." It was a temple that he would not occupy for thousands of years. Paul, in Colossians 1:26-27 refers to the "mystery that has been hidden for ages and generations, but is now disclosed to the saints...this mystery, which is Christ in you, the hope of glory."

It is not just Christ *with* you; it is Christ *in* you. The mystery hidden for ages is that God created you in his own likeness to be occupied by his Spirit.

Your body is the place of his presence.

And it is through your body that God reaches out to the world around you.

There are people in your life who will never hear the voice of God until you speak the Word to them.

There are people in your life who will never feel the touch of God until you reach out to them with the love and compassion of Christ.

There are people in your life who will never see the face of God until they see the light and life of Jesus in your eyes.

God didn't just save you so that you can be hidden away in

the ark while the rest of the world goes to hell. He saved you so that through the power of his Holy Spirit, you can reach out to a lost and needy world around you to bring grace and hope and salvation. You have a marvelous destiny in Christ.

> For we are God's workmanship, created in Christ Jesus to do good works, which God prepared in advance for us to do.
> (Ephesians 2:10)

And that is why the Bible tells us to offer our bodies to God. God wants to fill you afresh everyday with his Spirit so that he can use you to accomplish the purposes of heaven on earth.

> *The Lord Jesus Christ claims the use of your body, your whole being, your complete personality, so that as you give yourself to Him through the eternal Spirit, He may give Himself to you through the eternal Spirit, that all your activity as a human being on earth may be His activity in and through you; that every step you take, every word you speak, everything you do, everything you are, may be an expression of Christ, in you as man.*[1]
> *Major W. Ian Thomas (1914-)*

May our prayer today and everyday be:

Father, let your kingdom come and your will be done through me, right here, right now, on earth as it is in heaven.

Look through my eyes and tell me what you see.
Listen through my ears and tell me what you hear.
Touch through my hands and extend your grace and
  compassion to those I meet today.
Speak through my lips and brings words of hope
  and peace and forgiveness to a world in need
  of good news.
Holy Spirit, clothe yourself with my flesh.
Come and dwell in me today.

How do we offer our bodies to God? We'll look at that in the next three chapters.

HEAR MY PRAYER

Almighty, holy God, Creator of heaven and earth,
life is in Your breath, time is in Your hands,
creation is at the tip of Your tongue.
Where, indeed, will we build Your home?
In heaven? Heaven is Your chair.
On the earth? Earth is Your footrest.
And if we could build Your temple,
what would we make it with?
Wood that burns? Stone that crumbles?
Gold that melts? Gold is but the asphalt of heaven.
Indeed, how could we contain the uncontainable?
How could we give You anything of value?
You do not dwell in structures that are built by our hands.
Rather, You dwell in people who are broken by Your grace;
people whose hearts are mangers, not mansions;
people who have no worthiness
or righteousness of their own;
people who fear You as their God
and love You as their Father.
O Lord, give me a heart that looks like home to You.
Make me a temple for Your Holy Spirit.
Amen.

TEN

Heart Postures

> Therefore, I urge you, brothers, in view of God's mercy, to offer your bodies as living sacrifices, holy and pleasing to God—this is your spiritual act of worship. Do not conform any longer to the pattern of this world, but be transformed by the renewing of your mind... (Romans 12:1-2)

Romans 12:1-2 are about repentance—"do not conform any longer...but be transformed." Repentance is not a once in a lifetime commitment. It's not simply an apology with a promise to do better. Repentance is a whole new lifestyle.

Repentance is a determination to change the way we live—to stop, turn around, and head in a different direction.

Repentance is cooperating with God in the transformation of our character.

Repentance is a heart posture that is reflected in the choices we make.

Repentance is an act of worship.

We do not repent in order to earn forgiveness; we repent as a response to having already been forgiven. "While we were still sinners, Christ died for us" (Ro 5:8). He did not wait for us to clean up our act or behave ourselves properly. He died while we were hopelessly lost. When we discover that forgiveness is God's gift to us, it makes us want to change the way we live. He who has been forgiven much, loves much. Repentance, then, ceases to be an occasional act of desperation and instead becomes a continual expression of love and gratitude.

Repentance is absolutely impossible without the power of the Holy Spirit. Jesus said, “Apart from me you can do nothing” (Jn 15:5). But when we are empowered by his Holy Spirit, we can say with the Apostle Paul, “I can do all things through Christ who strengthens me” (Php 4:13, NKJV). That empowerment becomes available to us only as we surrender to God and invite him to dwell within us. And that empowerment is what enables us to live as holy people.

Matthew Henry wrote:

> *What God requires of us, he himself works in us, or it is not done. He that commands faith, holiness, and love, creates them by the power of his grace going along with his word, that he may have all the praise. Lord, give what thou commandest, and then command what thou pleasest.*[1]

To paraphrase Oswald Chambers, God doesn't make us holy by changing our character. He makes us holy by making us innocent before him.[2] Then, having been made holy, we begin the process of repentance—living out what the Holy Spirit is birthing in us.

Day by day, moment by moment, we learn to walk in his holiness, innocent and free before God.

Day by day, moment by moment, our character changes as the character of Christ is developing in us.

Day by day, moment by moment, "we are being transformed into his likeness with ever-increasing glory" (2Co 3:18).

Day by day, moment by moment, we are becoming what we already are—"holy and pleasing to God."

> You were taught, with regard to your former way of life, to put off your old self, which is being corrupted by its deceitful desires; to be made new in the attitude of your minds; and to put on the new self, created to be like God in true righteousness and holiness. (Ephesians 4:22-24)

We don't always see ourselves the way God sees us. Before we were born again, we didn't see how sinful we were. Now that we are born again, we don't see how holy we are. And in neither case do we see how beloved we are. Our poor-sightedness is not a new problem:

> *I regard myself as the most wretched of all men, stinking and covered with sores, and as one who has committed all sorts of crimes against his King. Overcome by remorse, I confess all my wickedness to Him, ask His pardon and abandon myself entirely to Him to do with as He will. But this King, filled with goodness and mercy, far from chastising me, lovingly embraces me, makes me eat at His table, serves me with His own hands, gives me the keys of His treasures and treats me as His favorite. He talks with me and is delighted with me in a thousand and one ways; He forgives me and relieves me of my principal bad habits without talking about them; I beg Him to*

make me according to His heart and always the more weak and despicable I see myself to be, the more beloved I am of God.[3]

Brother Lawrence of the Resurrection (1614-1691)

How do we live a lifestyle of repentance? Are there physical expressions that reflect the posture of a surrendered heart? Can we really, physically offer our bodies to God as living sacrifices, or is this just figurative language? To answer those questions, it will help us to look at what the Bible says about our bodies in the contexts of daily living and personal devotions. We'll do that in the next two chapters.

HEAR MY PRAYER

Thank You, Father, for the gift of holiness.
We are not Yours because we are holy;
we are holy because we are Yours.
Now help us to live as holy people.
Teach us to "purify ourselves from everything
that contaminates body and spirit,
perfecting holiness out of reverence for God."
And as we grow in Your holiness,
righteousness and faith,
may we bring glory, honor
and praise to Your name.
Amen

ELEVEN

Offer Your Body to God in Your Daily Living

> Do not offer the parts of your body to sin, as instruments of wickedness, but rather offer yourselves to God, as those who have been brought from death to life; and offer the parts of your body to him as instruments of righteousness. (Romans 6:13)

Here is a list of Scriptures (certainly not exhaustive, but enough to get you started) that will help you understand God's perspective on how you can offer your body to him on a daily basis as a spiritual act of worship. We will look at what the Bible says about your ears, your eyes, your mouth, and their relationship to your thoughts.

Your Ears

Let's begin with your ears. How can you offer your ears as a living sacrifice to God? Consider these words of instruction from Scripture:

> The heart of the discerning acquires knowledge;
> the ears of the wise seek it out. (Proverbs 18:15)

> Faith comes from hearing the message, and the message is heard through the word of Christ. (Romans 10:17)

> Apply your heart to instruction
> and your ears to words of knowledge. (Proverbs 23:12)

Does not the ear test words
as the tongue tastes food? (Job 12:11)

What do we allow ourselves to listen to? What kind of environment do we create for our ears? Is it an environment in which faith can be nurtured? Is it conducive to worship? We spit out foods that offend our sense of taste. What do we do with words that offend our hearing?

Perhaps our ears need to refine their sense of "taste."

Your Eyes

How can you offer your eyes to God as a living sacrifice? Here is what the Bible says:

I have made a covenant with my eyes
not to look lustfully at a girl. (Job 31:1)

Turn my eyes away from worthless things. (Psalm 119:37)

I will set before my eyes
no vile thing. (Psalm 101:3)

Vile means wicked, perverted, offensive to the senses, disgusting, cheap, degrading. What are we doing with our eyes? What do we allow ourselves to look at? I'm not just talking about pictures, but also about printed words and real life situations. What choices are we making that set us up for failure in this area?

This issue has special significance for those of us who are married men. The Apostle Peter tells us to treat our wives with respect, "so that nothing will hinder your prayers" (1Pe 3:7). There are few things more disrespectful that a man can do to his wife than to look lustfully at another woman. Not only will it impact his married life, it will also darken his thought life, and according to Peter, it will disable his prayer life. So, guys, if your prayers are being hindered, perhaps it has something to do with what you are doing with your eyes.

Of course, there are other applications for the Bible's instructions about our eyes. Not long ago a friend of mine gave me a book written by one of my favorite authors. This writer is a great storyteller: he travels the world and writes about his adventures. In my book, he's one of the funniest men alive. But this author also has a foul mouth—an excessively foul mouth. After reading three or four chapters, I found that I was repeatedly feeling stung by the author's crudeness. I finally stopped mid-sentence and thought, "Why am I reading this? What do I stand to gain by it, and is the gain worth the constant pricking of my conscience? I don't want those words in my mind or in my heart, because I don't want them coming out of my mouth. I don't want them coming out of my mouth because they are offensive to God and demeaning to my character." So I threw the book away.

Am I prudish or puritanical? I don't think so. I still think the guy is hilarious. I'm simply making a value judgment. And in my judgment, the value just isn't there anymore. It's not that I'm going through life with my eyes closed and my hands over my ears. I have simply decided to avoid avoidable situations. I have made a conscious choice to follow James' advice to "Get rid of all the moral filth and superfluous wickedness" in my life (Jas 1:21[1]). I've decided that I don't want to conform any longer to the pattern of the world. And I'm finding that God is transforming me by renewing my mind. He is changing the way I think.

The eyes and ears are the gateways to the soul. Guard the gates as though your life depended on it. Because it does.

Your Mouth

How can you offer your mouth as a living sacrifice? Again, let's see what the Bible has to say.

> Keep your tongue from evil
> and your lips from speaking lies.
> (Psalm 34:13)

> I said, "I will watch my ways
> and keep my tongue from sin;
> I will put a muzzle on my mouth
> as long as the wicked are in my presence."
> (Psalm 39:1)

> What goes into a man's mouth does not make him "unclean," but what comes out of his mouth, that is what makes him "unclean." (Matthew 15:11)

Rid yourselves of ... slander and filthy language from your lips. (Colossians 3:8)

Above all else, guard your heart,
for it is the wellspring of life.
Put away perversity from your mouth;
keep corrupt talk far from your lips.
(Proverbs 4:23-24)

Jesus taught us that our lips reveal the content of our hearts. "Out of the overflow of the heart the mouth speaks"(Mt 12:34). What do your lips reveal about the content of your heart? What are you filling your heart with that overflows from your lips?

Is your mouth full of…

Encouragement or criticism?
Mercy or anger?
Love or hatred?
Kindness or cursing?
Faith or doubt?
Peace or animosity?
Joy or hopelessness?

David prayed:

May the words of my mouth and the meditation
of my heart
be pleasing in your sight,
O Lord, my Rock and my Redeemer. (Psalm 19:14)

That's my prayer, too.

Your Thoughts

I know that your thoughts are not physical parts of your body. But they are inseparable from your body. Your thoughts both reflect and direct what you do with your eyes, your ears, and your mouth.

> In his pride the wicked does not seek him;
> in all his thoughts there is no room for God. (Psalm 10:4)

> Take captive every thought to make it obedient to Christ.
> (2Corinthians 10:5)

One of the best ways I have found to take every thought captive to Christ is to develop the habit of turning self-talk into God-talk. You know what self-talk is—it is the silent and secret conversations you have with yourself. But turning self-talk into God-talk can actually be a method of praying without ceasing. Throughout the day, whenever you have random thoughts of people or situations, try turning your thoughts into prayer. Rather than talk to yourself, talk to God. By doing this, you make room in your thoughts for God (Ps 10:4).

I started doing this several years ago and quickly developed the practice to a point where it is now almost subconscious. Where I used to catch myself in the middle of a daydream, it surprises me now how often I catch myself in the middle of a prayer.

Here are more scriptures about how to offer your thoughts to God as an act of worship:

Finally, brothers, whatever is true, whatever is noble, whatever is right, whatever is pure, whatever is lovely, whatever is admirable—if anything is excellent or praiseworthy—think about such things. (Philippians 4:8)

Set your minds on things above, not on earthly things.
(Colossians 3:2)

Therefore, prepare your minds for action; be self-controlled.
(1Peter 1:13)

Clothe yourselves with the Lord Jesus Christ, and do not think about how to gratify the desires of the sinful nature.
(Romans 13:14)

What exactly are "the desires of the sinful nature"? They include more than just lust or vengeance. The desires of the sinful nature also include selfish ambition, envy, conceit, pride, and jealousy.

So the question is, what am I doing with my thought-life? Am I taking my thoughts captive to Christ or are my thoughts imprisoning me? Do I dwell on hurtful memories or grievances? Am I keeping a record of wrongs committed against me? Do I let my mind wander into mine fields of anger or vengeance or lust? Do I allow my imagination to run wild after elaborate schemes and selfish ambitions? Are my aspirations driven by human will or are they in pursuit of God's will?

Am I thinking the way the world thinks or am I thinking with the mind of Christ?

I am learning to ask God every day to protect my mind and direct my thoughts. If I find myself thinking in ways that are offensive to God, I immediately ask his forgiveness and call out to him to purify my heart and mind. I invite the Holy Spirit to take control of my thoughts and to teach me to think with the mind of Christ so that I might know God's will in every situation.

Hear My Prayer

In light of Your kind mercy to me, dear Father,
I offer to You my whole self without reservation,
holding nothing back.
My body is now Your temple.
I am no longer my own; I was bought at a price.
Therefore, I will honor You with my body.
I will live as one who has been crucified with Christ,
and who lives again in Him,
through Him and for His glory.
I bring every thought captive to obedience to Christ.
I make a covenant with my eyes to keep them pure.
I offer You my hands and feet
for the service of Your ministry.
Come and fill me with Your Spirit, Lord.
Teach me to live a life
that is worthy of Your calling
and that conforms with
Your good, pleasing and perfect will.
Amen.

TWELVE

Offer Your Body to God in Your Personal Devotions

Begin at once; before you venture away from this quiet moment, ask your King to take you wholly into his service, and place all the hours of this day quite simply at his disposal, and ask him to make and keep you ready to do just exactly what he appoints. Never mind about tomorrow; one day at a time is enough. Try it today, and see if it is not a day of strange, almost curious peace, so sweet that you will be only too thankful when tomorrow comes to ask him to take it also.[1]

Francis Ridley Havergal (1836-1879)

I like to start my day with prayer and devotions. Some days I pray in my bedroom, some days in my office, and quite often in my car as I drive to work. I begin by thanking God for another day and for the blessings he has given to me. I also thank him for the challenges that lie ahead. I invite him to search my heart and to point out anything that is offensive to him. I ask him to forgive me and to wash me clean through the blood of Jesus. Then I invite him to fill me afresh with his Holy Spirit.

When we read in Judges 6:34 that the Holy Spirit came upon Gideon, it literally means that the Holy Spirit clothed himself with Gideon. So I invite the Holy Spirit to clothe himself with my flesh—to fully inhabit my "temple," and then to use me for that day to accomplish the purposes of heaven on earth.

The Bible speaks to us about how we can offer our bodies to God in our personal devotions. Let's look specifically at what the Scriptures teach us about singing, kneeling, and lifting our hands to God.

Singing

There are 139 verses of Scripture about singing to the Lord. (And of course, the Book of Psalms is a collection of 150 song lyrics.) Here are just a few of those verses:

> I will sing of the Lord's great love forever;
> with my mouth I will make your faithfulness known
> through all generations. (Psalm 89:1)

> I will sing to the Lord all my life;
> I will sing praise to my God as long as I live. (Psalm 104:33)

> Speak to one another with psalms, hymns and spiritual songs. Sing and make music in your heart to the Lord, always giving thanks to God the Father for everything, in the name of our Lord Jesus Christ. (Ephesians 5:19)

> Let the word of Christ dwell in you richly as you teach and admonish one another with all wisdom, and as you sing psalms, hymns and spiritual songs with gratitude in your hearts to God. (Colossians 3:16)

Jesus sang (Mt 26:30). Paul sang (Ac 16:25). The disciples sang (Mt 26:30). Moses sang (Ex 15:1). David sang (2Sa 22:1). Solomon sang (SS 1:1). Jonah sang (Jnh 2:9).

So singing must be important to God. And it must be important to us.

Did you ever notice that there is no musical notation in the Bible? Some people might say, "Well, that's because there was no method for writing music down." Exactly. But if God cared enough about the words to gift us with the ability to write them down, why didn't he also give us the ability to write music down when the Scriptures were first written? Perhaps it is because he knows that if music were in the Bible, then the music in the church today would still sound like a song-and-dance number from a Charlton Heston Bible movie, and all of the instruments in church would be trumpets, lyres and sackbuts. That'll fill up a Saturday night service!

But even though there are no melodies in the Bible, we are still told to sing to the Lord. In fact, David says, "Sing to the Lord a new song" (Ps 149:1). The song of worship keeps our hearts in a posture of praise. It reminds us of God's faithfulness, his kindness, his majesty, and above all, his presence.

Here's another great reason to sing to the Lord. 1Thessalonians 5:17 (NKJV) is one of the shortest verses in the Bible. It consists of just three words, but they speak volumes: "Pray without ceasing." How is that possible?

Sing.

If you take a close look at the lyrics of hymns and worship songs, you will find that many of them are written to God, not just about God; and as such, they are sung prayers. Consider, for example, "I Love You, Lord," "As the Deer," "Great is Thy

Faithfulness, "How Great Thou Art," and "Lord, I Lift Your Name on High." All of these songs are sung to God—they are prayers set to music.

So, how can you pray without ceasing? Keep a song in your heart. Sing to the Lord and let the song draw you deeper into prayer.[2]

Personally, I don't believe that singing in worship is optional. I think God wants us to sing, regardless of how well we think we do it. God gave you your voice. He delights in the sound of it. It is music to his ears. If he doesn't like it, he can change it. The Bible says make a joyful noise unto the Lord. So as long as it's joyful and noisy, you're on the right track! Sing to him.

Kneeling

> Come, let us bow down in worship,
> let us kneel before the Lord our Maker.
> (Psalm 95:6)

When I present myself to God in prayer, I often do so on my knees. Kneeling before God is a Biblical posture of submission. It is a physical demonstration of a spiritual reality. By bowing my knees I am bowing my heart and surrendering my will to God's sovereignty.

There are over 100 examples in Scripture of people kneeling in prayer and worship. Jesus prayed on his knees (Lk 22:41). Paul prayed on his knees (Eph 3:14). Peter prayed on his knees

(Ac 9:40). All the disciples and their families prayed on their knees (Ac 21:5). Ezra prayed on his knees (Ezr 9:5). Solomon prayed on his knees (2Ch 6:13). All of the Israelites prayed on their knees (2Ch 7:3). Daniel prayed on his knees—three times a day (Dan 6:10).

So I pray on my knees.

While I am on my knees, I also lift my hands to God. This brings up an important issue—lifted hands.

Lifting your hands.

Why do some people lift their hands to God when they sing or pray? (Relax, I'm a Presbyterian, so you can trust me on this one.)

It is important for us to look closely at the practice of lifting hands to God because it can so easily be misunderstood. I hear some folks say, "Oh, that's just fine for those people, but we don't do that kind of thing at our church. It's much too showy." On the other hand, I hear people say, "You're not really worshiping God until you do it our way." But I think the decisions we make in both private and congregational worship should be informed decisions—informed not just by tradition nor by emotion, but informed by the Word of God. After all, if we're worshiping God, shouldn't we find out if he has any preferences?

Let's see what the Bible has to say about lifting our hands to God:

I will praise you as long as I live,
and in your name I will lift up my hands.
(Psalm 63:4)

I call to you, O Lord, everyday;
I spread out my hands to you.
(Psalm 88:9)

Lift up your hands in the sanctuary
and praise the Lord. (Psalm 134:2)

Ezra praised the Lord, the great God; and all the people lifted their hands and responded, "Amen! Amen!" (Nehemiah 8:6)

Let us lift up our heart with our hands
unto God in the heavens.
(Lamentations 3:41, KJV)

I fell on my knees with my hands spread out to the Lord my God and prayed. (Ezra 9:5-6)

[Solomon] knelt down before the whole assembly of Israel and spread out his hands toward heaven. (2Chronicles 6:13)

I want men everywhere to lift up holy hands in prayer.
(1Timothy 2:8)

"Everyday," David says in Psalm 88:9, "I call to you and spread out my hands to you."

Every day.

Look at your hands. They aren't going to hurt you; just look at them for a moment. Magnificent, aren't they? Who gave us our hands? God gave them to us. What do we do with our hands? Well, we work with our hands. We feed ourselves with our hands. We play with our hands. We give gifts and receive gifts with our hands. We show affection with our hands. We also fight with our hands. We sin with our hands.

Why are we so hesitant to worship God with our hands?

Lifting our hands to God is a Biblical posture of prayer. It is another physical demonstration of a spiritual truth. Just as we bow our hearts when we bow our knees, so we lift our hearts when we lift our hands (Lam 3:41).

By kneeling before God and lifting our hands to him, we are presenting our bodies to God as a spiritual act of worship.

You may have never done these things before, or you may do them everyday. But ultimately, it is the posture of your heart that counts. The Father is looking for worshipers who will worship him in spirit and in truth (Jn 4:23). God wants honesty, not showmanship. You can be kneeling on the outside, but standing on the inside. You can have your hands raised outwardly in praise, while on the inside, your fists are clenched in defiance. In Isaiah 29:13 the Lord warns:

> These people come near to me with their mouth
> and honor me with their lips,
> but their hearts are far from me.
> Their worship of me
> is made up only of rules taught by men.

So what is the condition of your heart today—hard and brittle or soft and pliable?

Let me make a suggestion. Tonight when you are getting ready for bed, kick one of your shoes under the bed. Then, tomorrow morning when you are down on your knees looking for your shoe, take a moment to give God what he is looking for.[3] Open your heart, open your hands, and offer your body to him as a living sacrifice.

A Daily Prayer of Surrender

There is an old method of prayer that I have borrowed from the Quakers. I use it often as a physical reminder of the posture of my heart. This kind of prayer involves the use of my hands to symbolize my interaction with God.

As I pray, I present my requests to God with my palms turned up, about waist high. Then I release my concerns to God with my palms turned down. Finally I receive God's grace with my palms turned up again. Then I repeat the process, presenting, releasing and receiving, all through the prayer of faith.

The words of the following prayer are mine, but the Quaker method is what I want to demonstrate to you. These words are only meant to get you started. Use your own words as you talk to God.

Remember, God is not impressed with eloquence.

He just wants honesty.

And what he wants most from you in prayer is *you.*[4]

Let's pray:

With palms turned up:

Father, I come to you today in Jesus' name. Thank you for your kindness that has brought me to another day. Thank you for your love and faithfulness. Thank you for accepting me as I am and for transforming me into the likeness of Christ. I present myself before you, body, soul and spirit. I bring you my strengths and my weaknesses, my successes and my failures, my hopes and my fears, my dreams and my nightmares.

With palms turned down:

Now, Father, by faith I release all of these things into your lap of grace and I surrender to your sovereignty. I cast all of my cares upon you, and I pray, let your will be done in my life today.

With palms turned up:

Father, I now receive from you all that your grace will afford to me today: strength for my weaknesses, peace for my fears, forgiveness for my sins and the grace to forgive those who sin against me. I look to you to meet all of my needs. Guide my steps, direct my thoughts, and protect me from the evil one. I invite you to fill me today with your Holy Spirit. Let me be an extension of your grace and mercy to the world around me. Use my life, I pray, to bring glory to your name.

Amen.

HEAR MY PRAYER

When You formed man in Your image
out of the dust of the ground,
You were building a temple.
And as a creature of dust, I too am a temple.
You have placed my name above the door
and now You stand at the door and knock,
waiting for me to invite You in.
Lord of heaven, come and be
Lord of this piece of earth.
Come and fill this temple with the
living breath of Your Holy Spirit.
Make it a place of worship.
Find Your rest within its walls.
Be enthroned on my praises.
Amen.

SECTION THREE

GOD ENCOUNTERS

Then you will be able to test and approve what God's will is— his good, pleasing and perfect will.

THIRTEEN

HEARING FROM GOD

Speak, Lord, for your servant is listening. (1Samuel 3:9)

Has God ever spoken to you? Would you recognize his voice if he did? Some people say that God no longer speaks. How sad it must be to worship a God who won't talk to you.

To believe that God no longer speaks is an unreasonable proposition. Does it make any sense that the God who created us, the God who gave his very own Son to die for us, the God who is so intimate that he actually dwells inside us by his own Spirit now has nothing to say to us?

To believe that God no longer speaks is a frightening proposition. Throughout Scripture, when God is present, he is speaking. If God no longer speaks, is he no longer present?

To believe that God no longer speaks is a hopeless proposition. If God no longer speaks, then what makes us think he is listening?

God still speaks.

He speaks to us through the Scriptures, through the wise counsel of other brothers and sisters in Christ, through providence bestowed or withheld, through circumstances, opportunities and closed doors, and through the still, small voice of his Spirit speaking to our consciences, bringing conviction, comfort or correction. But always, God's speaking is consistent with the

Scriptures. He will never violate his own written Word.

A.W. Tozer wrote:

> *God is forever seeking to speak Himself out to His creation. He is, by His nature continuously articulate. He fills the world with His speaking voice.*[1]

Some people say, "Well, God has never spoken to me." But I must ask, "What have you been trying to hear?" For whose benefit have you been listening?

I believe that hearing *from* God begins with the desire to hear *for* God.

Far too often, we come to God with specific expectations. We want to hear about a particular subject. So we search the Scriptures looking for just the right verse to justify our preconceived position. Or we seek the counsel of one person after another until we hear what we want to hear. But that is not the way of a servant.

A servant listens to his master for the master's benefit, not his own. He receives instruction, correction, and encouragement for the furthering of his master's will. He hears *from* his master out of a desire to hear *for* his master.

The servant's only question is, "What message does my Lord have for his servant?" (Jos 5:14). The servant's prayer is, "Not my will, but your will be done" (see Mt 26:39).

We do not worship a silent God. He is always speaking.

We just need to learn how to listen.

HEAR MY PRAYER

Father, I want to live a life that pleases You.
I want to walk through each day depending
on Your power, looking for Your hand,
listening for the still, small voice
of Your guidance.
Use me for Your kingdom's purposes.
Nudge me into greater acts of faith.
Call me to a deeper level of trust.
Soften my heart, O Lord, so that I may live
worthy of Your calling and fulfill
Your highest purpose for my life.
Amen.

FOURTEEN

CONVERSATIONAL PRAYER

As in Paradise, God walks in the Holy Scriptures, seeking man.[1]

St. Ambrose (339-397)

If Ambrose was right—if God is looking for me in the Scriptures—then the question I must answer is, "What will I say to him when he finds me there?"

◆

I have been walking with the Lord all of my life. I received Jesus as my Savior when I was six years old, and I have never wandered from the faith. But it wasn't until I was 38 years old that I finally learned a way to read the Bible and pray that revolutionized my life.

Up to that point, I had tried to be faithful in prayer and Bible reading, but my success came in fits and starts. I wanted to be a good Christian—a man of the Word and a man of prayer. I was told I should be, anyway; and I was given the impression that my life was supposed to imitate the lifestyles of the great saints of the faith.

But their stories seemed to be one example after another of a lifestyle that I could not achieve. These were people who spent hours everyday in their prayer closets, and even more hours everyday in the Word. They read through the whole Bible every year. They were spiritual giants—God's best friends. And I came to believe that if I wanted to be a spiritual giant, I too had to read and pray for hours a day.

So I made a resolution to myself and to God that I would get up every morning before sunrise and pray for an hour.

My experience, however, was a dismal failure.

First of all, I'm not a morning person. Nevertheless, I wanted to "beat my body daily," as I seemed to remember the Apostle Paul saying somewhere. So I got up at 5am, stumbled downstairs in the dark to the living room, stubbed my toe on the coffee table, and said something that gave me another reason to pray. Then I fell to my knees and travailed for what seemed an eternity only to find that it had not been more than 5 minutes. So I prayed with even more fervency and "gnashing of teeth, " but the results were always the same.

Trying to corral my thoughts was like trying to herd cats.

Fighting off sleep was like skiing in front of an avalanche.

It was a hopeless cause.

I was a helpless case.

I felt small and weak.

As for my Bible reading program, I committed to read through the entire Bible in a year. There are 31,101 verses in the Bible. To make it all the way through in a year meant I had to read 85 verses each day. That didn't sound like too much. But after two weeks, I found myself several days behind schedule.

Strangely, the Bible began to morph into a source of guilt rather than a source of comfort. By the fourth week, it sat on the night table and stared at me, scolding me for being such an utter failure.

"You can't even make it through 85 verses—just 3 chapters a day. What a wimp!"

I felt smaller and weaker.

Does any of this sound familiar? I knew that my experience was in no way unique, and I found both comfort and sadness in that knowledge. Comfort in knowing that I wasn't the only one who struggled and failed; sadness to know that thousands and indeed millions of other Christians also struggle and fail. I was certain there must be a way to approach the spiritual disciplines that would turn drudgery to joy.

Then one day I stopped and said to myself, "Where in the Bible does it say that I'm supposed to read through the Bible in a year? Whose idea was this, anyway? This can't be what the Lord has in mind. I love God with all of my heart. But how can I have a deep, personal relationship with him when my attempts at pleasing him fall so far short of the mark?"

It was about that time that I discovered a book titled, *Spiritual Disciplines for the Christian Life,* by Donald Whitney. It's the best book on the spiritual disciplines that I have read. In his book, Whitney quotes a passage from the diary of George Muller. Muller was a great man of prayer who lived in England in the 1800's. His life is a fascinating study in faith. This quote, though lengthy, is packed with meaning. It opened my eyes to a new, but oh so obvious approach to my devotional life with God:

Before this time my practice had been...as an habitual thing, to give myself to prayer after having dressed in the morning. Now, I saw that the most important thing was to give myself to the reading of God's Word, and to meditation on it, that by means of the Word of God, whilst meditating on it, my heart might be brought into [experiential] communion with the Lord.

I began therefore to meditate on the New Testament from the beginning, early in the morning...searching as it were into every verse to get blessing out of it; not for the sake of public ministry...but for the sake of obtaining food for my own soul.

The result I have found to be almost invariably this, that after a few minutes my soul has been led to confession, or to thanksgiving, or to intercession, or to supplication; so that, though I did not, as it were, give myself to prayer, but to meditation, yet it turned almost immediately more or less to prayer. When thus I have been for a while making intercession or supplication, or have given thanks, I go on to the next words or verse, turning all, as I go on, into prayer for myself or others, as the Word may lead to it...

The difference, then, between my former practice and my present one is this: formerly, when I rose, I began to pray as soon as possible, and generally spent all my time till breakfast in prayer...But what was the result? I often spent a quarter of an hour, or half an hour, or even an hour on my knees before being conscious to myself of having derived comfort, encouragement, humbling of soul, etc.; and often, after having suffered much from

> *wandering of mind for the first ten minutes, or quarter of an hour, or even half an hour...*
>
> *I scarcely ever suffer now in this way. For my heart being nourished by the truth, being brought into [experiential] fellowship with God, I speak to my Father and to my Friend (vile though I am, and unworthy of it) about the things that He has brought before me in His precious Word. It often now astonishes me that I did not sooner see this point...And yet now, since God has taught me this point, it is as plain to me as anything that the first thing the child of God has to do morning by morning is to obtain food for his inner man.*
>
> *Now what is food for the inner man? Not prayer, but the Word of God; and here again, not the simple reading of the Word of God, so that it passes through our minds, just as water passes through a pipe, but considering what we read, pondering over it and applying it to our hearts.*[2]

With those words, everything fell into place. I finally understood the relational nature of the spiritual disciplines of prayer and Bible reading. They are two parts of a conversation. A deep conversation. And, as in any conversation, it is most helpful if both parties are discussing the same subject.

In the past, I would come to God in prayer with my list of needs, wants and concerns, and then rush off before he could get a word in edgewise. I was doing all of the talking.

But now I understood that conversational prayer begins with listening. And listening begins with the Word of God. In other words, I am learning to let God start the conversation. Before I pray, I turn to the Scriptures to find out what is on God's heart. I let the Bible feed my thoughts and let my thoughts flow into prayer.

Prayer, then, becomes a response to what God wants to talk about.

If he speaks words of correction, I respond with confession, apology and repentance.

If he speaks words of comfort, I respond with thanksgiving.

If he speaks words of instruction, I respond with submission.

If he speaks words of hope, I respond with joyful praise.

In any case, I find out first what is on his mind and then I let his thoughts direct my prayers. My prayer list still gets prayed for. But I am no longer handing God his "to do" list for the day. Instead, I am handing *myself* to God and inviting him "to do" his will.

A profound change has taken place since I learned to pray this way. I still pray to God as my Father, as my Lord and as my King. But I also talk to him now as my Friend.

Peter Kreeft wrote in his book, *Reading and Praying the New Testament:*

> *Reading and praying the [Scriptures] is putting yourself in God's way, standing in the great waterfall of living water. If you stand in the street, you'll get hit by a truck. If you stand in the word, you'll get kissed by God. It is God's mistletoe.*[3]

Hear My Prayer

Almighty God, when I seek You in humility,
You respond in majesty.
So let this be the pattern of my prayer:
that I will first seek to understand You,
then seek to be understood by You;
that I will first seek to know Your concerns,
then seek to make my concerns known to You.
I pray, Lord, that You will always
find in me a listening ear —
that I will be one in whom You can
entrust the secret of Your kingdom.
Amen.

FIFTEEN

Reading God's Mind, Praying God's Thoughts

Approach the Bible not only as a book which was once spoken, but a book which is now speaking. God's speaking is in the continuous present.[1]

A.W. Tozer (1897-1963)

Reading the Bible is reading God's mind. The Bible is a personal letter from God to you. It reveals his deepest thoughts and feelings about you.

You can be absolutely confident that he cares about you, because you have his Word on it.

You can know without a doubt that he has a plan for your life, because you have his Word on it.

He knows your struggles, he feels your heartache, he hears your prayers, he shares your joys, he takes great delight in you—you have his Word on it.

God has given us the Bible as a means of knowing him and enjoying his presence. It is a catalyst for worship. The Scriptures tell us not just what God did but how God does things. They are the primary means of hearing his voice and discovering his will. They reveal to us his unchanging nature and character.

The Scriptures are the starting points of our conversations with God. So how do you let the Bible direct your prayer life?

Let me suggest a method:

Read for depth, not for distance.

Reading the Bible for distance is like skipping a stone across the surface of the stream behind Sutter's Mill. It's fun to impress ourselves or our friends with how far we can skip the stone, but we never stop to explore anything beneath the water's surface. We fail to recognize just how deep and clear the water is. We don't see the life teeming in its depths. And we miss out on the gold nuggets lying in the streambed.

But reading for depth instead of distance gives us the opportunity to search for and discover the untold riches that await us. The longer we look beneath the surface, the more we see, and the more we see, the richer we become.

In *Spiritual Disciplines for the Christian Life*, Don Whitney says that reading the Word is like making a cup of tea: You are the cup of water and the Word is the tea bag. Reading the passage once is like dipping the tea bag into the water one time. Not much happens to the water. But if you immerse the bag and let it steep in the water, the water will soon absorb all of the flavor and aroma and color of the tea.

This kind of reading is called "meditative reading" of Scripture. Meditative Scripture reading is reading for depth, not for distance.

To a lot of people, meditation sounds strange and New Age-y, like something "those people" in California would do, probably in groups—empty their minds, twist their bodies, and get in touch with some kind of cosmic weirdness.

But true Biblical meditation means to think deeply on a passage of Scripture, to fill your mind with it, to look at it from different angles, like a jeweler examining the various facets of a stone.

When I started to read the Bible meditatively, I began to experience tremendous changes in my life:

- *My thought life changed.* I struggled far, far less with lust and temptation.
- *My passions changed.* I found myself becoming more patient and compassionate.
- *My outlook changed.* I began to see circumstances, challenges and opportunities through a lens of Scripture. I found that the Scriptures were taking root so deeply in my soul through meditative reading that they became the filters for my point of view.
- *My prayer life changed.* It became conversational, rather than one sided. I let God start the conversation through his Word, and prayed according to what I heard him saying in the Scriptures I was studying.
- *My values changed.* I found that I was developing an insatiable appetite for the Word of God. I turned off the TV. I put away the novels and the news magazines. I even turned off the car stereo and devoted all of my spare time to conversation with God. My car became a private sanctuary of prayer and worship.

- *My motivation changed.* This may sound funny, but I stopped trying to *do* something and simply began to *be* something—or perhaps I should say, "someone." I stopped reading and praying for the sake of duty to God, and instead began reading and praying for the sake of friendship with God. I found myself, as John Piper says, "wasting time with God."

And herein lay the greatest surprise of all: what used to be minutes that seemed like hours, now became hours that seemed like minutes. I lost all sense of time when I lost myself in meditative reading and prayer.

I am a very different person today than I was just a few short years ago, and the primary cause of the change has been the meditative reading of Scripture.

Perhaps I can best explain my process of meditative Scripture reading with a word picture. One of my favorite things to do on a beautiful, sunny, Southern California day is to go for a long drive, often with no particular destination in mind. I generally find myself navigating toward either the coastline or the mountains. In any event, the purpose of the drive is to immerse myself in my surroundings and forget about everything else.

There are six simple steps for this kind of drive:

1. Fill your tank. You can't make the trip if you're out of gas.
2. Choose your road. It may be on old favorite that you've

traveled many times. Or it may be a new road that you never noticed before.

3. Slow down and take in the beauty of your surroundings. What colors do you see? Look at the plants and wildlife. Smell the air. Listen.

4. Pull off the road at a scenic viewpoint. Stop the car, step into the scene, and take a look around.

5. Take a picture of yourself. How do you look in this setting?

6. Send home a postcard. Tell the family where you went today—what you saw, what you heard, what you learned.

This is how it applies to meditative reading:

1. Fill your tank. Before you open your Bible, take a moment to open your heart and ask God to fill you afresh with his Holy Spirit. The Bible says that God's thoughts can only be understood by God's Spirit. It is the Spirit of God abiding in you that makes his Word come alive to you.

> No one knows the thoughts of God except the Spirit of God. We have not received the spirit of the world but the Spirit who is from God, that we may understand what God has freely given us...The man without the Spirit does not accept the things that come from the Spirit of God, for they are foolishness to him, and he cannot understand them, because they are spiritually discerned...But we have the mind of Christ.
>
> (1Corinthians 2:11-12,14,16)

Now you are ready to listen. You can open your Bible in faith, believing that God will speak to you from his Word.

2. Choose your road. Select your passage. It may be an old favorite that you've read many times. It may even be the passage you read yesterday. Or it may be a new "road" you've never explored before. I'm not suggesting that you simply open your Bible at random with your eyes closed and drop your finger on the page. Give it more thought and prayer than that. Consider, instead, working your way through a book of the Bible, or re-reading the chapter from which your pastor preached last weekend.

3. Slow down and take in the beauty of your surroundings. If you drive too fast, you will miss out on a lot. This drive is not a race—it's an exploration. Remember, you're reading for depth, not for distance. So take your time.

As you read your passage of scripture, slow down and enjoy the "scenery." What else is going on in the surrounding verses? What are you discovering about God's nature in the text? What are you seeing that you may have not seen before? What is the Author's train of thought? What is the significance of the words he used?

Go slower.

You might even want to turn around and drive back up the page to get a closer look at something you missed the first time you passed by.

Read the passage as though you were writing it. How long would it take you to write those words by hand? Read them that slowly, out loud to yourself. Romans 10:17 says that faith comes through hearing the word, so "read with your ears" and hear the word of the Lord.

Martin Luther said:

I study my Bible as I gather apples. First, I shake the whole tree that the ripest might fall. Then I shake each limb, and when I have shaken each limb, I shake each branch and every twig. Then I look under every leaf.[2]

That is how to read the Bible.

4. Pull over at a scenic viewpoint. For example, consider this scenic viewpoint in Colossians chapter 3 verse 16.

"Let the word of Christ dwell in you richly..."

Stop and focus on these words for awhile. Read the phrase several times and emphasize the words differently each time you read them. For instance, you might read the verse this way: "LET the word of Christ dwell in you richly..." By emphasizing "let" you realize that you have a definite choice in the matter. It's as though the Word of Christ were waiting for your permission to enter your heart. So open your heart and invite the Word to do its work in you.

Next you might read it: "Let the word of Christ DWELL in you richly..." Dwell, not just visit, or stop by for a quick "hello," but let it dwell in you, take up residence, make itself at home.

Then you might read it: "Let the word of Christ dwell in you RICHLY..." Richly is a meaningful word here. It takes my mind back to the tea illustration. The longer the tea bag "dwells" in the water, the richer the tea becomes, until the water finally absorbs all of the flavor and aroma and color of the tea. Each time you read the verse, or even a phrase, it takes on a deeper, richer meaning.

After you've read the verse or phrase with different emphases, try to put it into your own words. Don't worry, this is not heresy. You are simply letting God know that you are listening by telling him what you just heard him say.

I confess that I tend to be a speed-listener. Unfortunately, the person most often victimized by my reckless listening is the person I love the very most—my wife. Lynnda is a delightful conversationalist. She absorbs herself in the person she is talking to. She hears every word; she catches every nuance. I, on the other hand, want to skip over the details and get to the point. The result, as you can guess, is disastrous.

Listening too fast, like driving too fast, can cause serious accidents and leave innocent victims scattered along the roadside. Speed-listening puts my life and relationships at risk. So I am trying to learn to slow down and listen carefully, thoughtfully and sensitively. I've found it to be most helpful if I make it clear that I am listening by summarizing or restating to Lynnda in my own words what Lynnda has said to me. Just knowing that I am going to do that makes me listen all the more closely.

I often take this same approach as I read the Scriptures. I will say back to God in my own words what I heard him say to me through his. For example, I might rephrase Colossians 3:16 this way:

> Permit, allow, make room for and welcome the Word of Christ to set up its residence in you—a beautiful, fully equipped, permanent home filled with the texture and color and aroma of the Word itself. Let it dwell in you richly, deeply, profoundly, abundantly.

5. Take a picture of yourself before you move on. The Bible tells us that the Word of God is, among other things, both a mirror and a light for our souls. So before I leave this Colossians passage, I ask myself, "What do I look like in this mirror? In the light of this verse, what faults or flaws are being revealed to me that were once hidden in darkness?" Or to get back to our word picture, what do I look like in this setting? Does the Word of Christ actually dwell in me richly, deeply, profoundly, abundantly? Or is it poverty stricken and neglected in my life—or worse yet, have I left it shivering on the back porch?

Taking a picture of yourself will help you remember what you experienced on your drive. And it will serve as a great conversation starter with other people who have visited the same road, or even with those who have never been there at all.

6. Send home a postcard. This is your prayer. Tell the Father where you were today, what you saw, what you heard, what you learned. It's at this point that my reading begins to turn to deep and serious prayer. Sometimes it is a prayer of confession. Sometimes it is a prayer of thanks. It might be a prayer of intercession for someone else. Or it might be a sung prayer of praise to God.

The point is that God is leading me in prayer. He is directing the conversation. By praying through the Scriptures, I am now praying God's thoughts back to God. I am, in a very real sense, agreeing with God in prayer.

You may find it helpful to write your prayers in a journal or even in the margin of your Bible. If you write your prayers, you might also want to date them. In this way, your written prayers will serve as memorials to your walk with God. They will be permanent reminders of when and how you encountered God, and how you responded to him in worship.

Some days my "drive" through the Scriptures may only cover a few verses. Other days, I make it through a few chapters, reading, thinking and praying as I go. But always I find that my memories of the "drive" stay with me for the rest of the day. They are not distant or vague memories that quickly fade; rather, they become continual impulses to talk with God.

My prayer life, then, is no longer boxed in to a specific, limited time frame. Instead, I find myself drawn into deeper conversation with God throughout the entire day. My prayers are not prayed out loud, unless I'm alone. Usually, they aren't more than a whisper. But I am conversing with God, nonetheless.

Thomas de Witt Talmage wrote:

> *God puts his ear so closely down to your lips that he can hear your faintest whisper. It is not God away off up yonder; it is God away down here, close up—so close up that when you pray to him, it is more a kiss than a whisper.*[3]

My conversations with God make me more aware of his continual presence. I have begun to experience and understand what Brother Lawrence described over 300 years ago in *The Practice of the Presence of God:*

> *I keep myself in his presence by simple attentiveness and a loving gaze upon God—or to put it more clearly, an habitual, silent and secret conversation of my soul with God.*[4]

"An habitual, silent and secret conversation." That is the way of a worshiper. And it is the secret to friendship with God.

◆

Are you looking for God? God is looking for worshipers. His invitation to friendship is open and genuine. Will you take him up on his offer? Will you give yourself to him in worship?

Let's take one more look at Romans 12:1-2, the scenic viewpoint of this book. This time, I've put it in my own words to let God know I am listening:

> Therefore, keeping in mind that God is merciful—that forgiveness is his natural inclination—it is his "default setting"—tell God he can have your body to live in. Trade in your agenda for his. He has already made you holy—you are just what he is looking for. And don't hold on to old thought patterns and habits. Let go of worthless idols and distractions. Don't try to be like everyone else anymore. Instead, let God, who is predisposed to forgive, make a new person out of you by giving you a new way of thinking. Then you will be able to try out his will for your life—his way of doing things. You will start thinking like he thinks. And when you've tried it, you'll find that it is incredible—it's not just good, its more than pleasing—it's absolutely perfect!

HEAR MY PRAYER

O Holy God, write Your Word
on the tablet of my life.
May it flood my heart and shine its light of truth
into every dark corner of my conscience.
May it enlighten my eyes and be the filter
through which I see all things.
May it fill my mind so that all of my thoughts
will be captive to obedience to Christ.
May it direct my steps into
Your good, pleasing and perfect will.
May it guide my hands into
the work of the ministry.
May it guard the doorway of my life so
that all of my comings and goings may pass
under the scrutiny of Your divine wisdom.
May Your Word, O God,
be the constant employer
of my spirit, soul and body.
Amen.

NOTES, CREDITS, ETC.

Chapter One:

1. Author's paraphrase.
2. Matthew Henry's insights on Psalm 25:14, from *A Commentary on the Whole Bible*, Fleming H. Revell Company.
3. This marvelous insight came from my good friend, Pastor Joseph Garlington.

Pg. 12 This prayer is from *The NIV Worship Bible*, Pg. 828; Maranatha! Publishing/Zondervan

Chapter Two:

Pg. 20 This prayer is from *The NIV Worship Bible*, Pg. 1489; Maranatha! Publishing/Zondervan

Chapter Three:

1. Matthew Henry, Quoted from *The NIV Worship Bible*, Pg. 6; Maranatha! Publishing/Zondervan

Pg. 25 This prayer is from *The NIV Worship Bible*, Pg. 1570; Maranatha! Publishing/Zondervan

Chapter Four:

1. I wish I could say that this statement is my own, but it isn't. I quite brazenly stole it from my friend, James Ryle. It's from his sermon, "The Greatest Promise Ever Made by the Greatest Promise Keeper Who Ever Lived," first preached at a Promise Keepers' conference in Knoxville, TN in 1997.

Pg. 36 This prayer is from *The NIV Worship Bible*, Pg. 1588; Maranatha! Publishing/Zondervan

Chapter Five:

1. The concept of the father as the prodigal was first suggested to me by my pastor, Mark Roberts, in his book, *After I Believe*, 2002, Baker Books. Mark discovered it in *The Waiting Father: Sermons on the Parables of Jesus*, by Helmut Thielicke, translated by John Doberstein, 1959, Harper.

Pg. 45 This prayer is from *The NIV Worship Bible*, Pg. 1515; Maranatha! Publishing/Zondervan

Chapter Six:

1. Matthew Henry's insights on Isaiah 6:1-4, from *A Commentary on the Whole Bible*, Fleming H. Revell Company.
2. C. S. Lewis, from *Mere Christianity*, 1952 Macmillan Publishing. Reprinted by permission of Harper Collins Publishing.

Pg. 55 This prayer is from *The NIV Worship Bible*, Pg. 1301; Maranatha! Publishing/Zondervan

Chapter Seven:

1. Izaak Walton, Quoted from *The NIV Worship Bible*, Pg. 522; Maranatha! Publishing/Zondervan

Pg. 64 This prayer is from *The NIV Worship Bible*, Pg. 1602; Maranatha! Publishing/Zondervan

Chapter Eight:

Pg. 73 This prayer is from *The NIV Worship Bible*, Pg. 217; Maranatha! Publishing/Zondervan

Chapter Nine:

1. Major W. Ian Thomas, from *The Saving Life of Christ*, 1961, 1978, Zondervan.

Pg. 79 This prayer is from *The NIV Worship Bible*, Pg. 996; Maranatha! Publishing/Zondervan

Chapter Ten:

1. Matthew Henry's insights on Genesis 1:8, from *A Commentary on the Whole Bible*, Fleming H. Revell Company.
2. Oswald Chambers, paraphrased from *My Utmost For His Highest*, September 8. Discovery House Publishers.
3. Brother Lawrence of the Resurrection, Quoted from *The NIV Worship Bible*, Pg. 1581; Maranatha! Publishing/Zondervan

Pg. 85 This prayer is from *The NIV Worship Bible*, Pg. 157; Maranatha! Publishing/Zondervan

Chapter Eleven:

1. Author's paraphrase.

Pg. 95 This prayer is from *The NIV Worship Bible*, Pg. 1522; Maranatha! Publishing/Zondervan

Chapter Twelve:

1. Francis Ridley Havergal, Quoted from *The NIV Worship Bible*, Pg. 1582; Maranatha! Publishing/Zondervan
2. I first encountered this idea of singing as a method of "praying without ceasing" in a sermon by my former pastor, Jack Hayford, when I was a teenager. If anything else in this book sounds even vaguely like Pastor Jack (and I hope it does) it's because he has had the greatest influence in my spiritual formation. If you tore down the "temple" called Buddy Owens, you would find Jack Hayford's signature scrawled in the foundation.
3. This is another great idea that I stole from a friend. It was Bob Horner from Campus Crusade Ministries that I first heard make the "shoe under the bed" suggestion.
4. Once again, I have borrowed a phrase from a dear friend, Robert Bakke. Quoted from *The NIV Worship Bible*, Pg.1653; Maranatha! Publishing/Zondervan

Pg. 106 This prayer is from *The NIV Worship Bible*, Pg. 5; Maranatha! Publishing/Zondervan

Chapter Thirteen:

1. A.W. Tozer, from *The Pursuit of God*, 1942, 1982 Christian Publications

Pg. 111 This prayer is from *The NIV Worship Bible*, Pg. 1596; Maranatha! Publishing/Zondervan

Chapter Fourteen:

1. St. Ambrose, Quoted from *The NIV Worship Bible*, Pg. 6; Maranatha! Publishing/Zondervan
2. George Muller, Quoted from *Spiritual Disciplines of the Christian Life*, © 1991 by Donald S. Whitney, Nav Press. I cannot speak highly enough of Whitney's book. It changed my life, and I am deeply grateful to its author. Whitney reprinted the Muller quote from *Spiritual Secrets of George Muller*, © 1985 by Roger Steer. American rights granted by Harold Shaw Publishers.
3. Peter Kreeft, from *Reading and Praying the New Testament,* 1992, Servant Publications

Pg. 119 This prayer is from *The NIV Worship Bible*, Pg. 1190; Maranatha! Publishing/Zondervan

Chapter Fifteen:

1. A.W. Tozer, from *The Pursuit of God*, 1942, 1982 Christian Publications
2. Martin Luther, Quoted from *The Classics Devotional Bible*, Pg. 241; Zondervan
3. Thomas de Witt Talmage, Quoted from *The NIV Worship Bible*, Pg. 656; Maranatha! Publishing/Zondervan
4. Brother Lawrence of the Resurrection, from *The Practice of the Presence of God*, translated by John J. Delaney, 1977, Doubleday

Pg. 133 This prayer is from *The NIV Worship Bible*, Pg. 238; Maranatha! Publishing/Zondervan

Thanks:

To Lynnda, my wife, for your unceasing love and kindness.

To Pete, for your great friendship and encouragement through the years.

To Lela Gilbert, my editor and friend.

To Bradley Grose and Terry DeGraff, for your many hours of hard work.

To the team at Maranatha! for your patience and your prayers.

To my parents, Jimmy and Carol Owens, for "training up a child in the way that he should go."

But most of all, to Tom and Randy for seeing more than my limited vision could take in. Thank you for your trust, your hope, your perseverance, and your friendship.

About the Author

Buddy Owens, General Editor of *The NIV Worship Bible*, has been with Maranatha! Music for 15 years. He is a national conference speaker for Promise Keepers and other church leadership conferences, teaching on the role of worship in a believer's life; and he is a frequent guest speaker at various churches, theological seminaries and Bible colleges. Buddy has also represented Maranatha! as a worship and programming consultant with Promise Keepers, Billy Graham Evangelistic Association, Luis Palau Evangelistic Association, United States Armed Forces Chaplains' Board, and the Nationally Broadcast Concert of Prayer. Buddy, his wife Lynnda and their four children live in Southern California.